Encounter in the Forest

Once, as I walked through thick forest in a downpour, I suddenly saw a chimp hunched in front of me. Quickly I stopped. Then I heard a sound from above. I looked up and there was a big chimp there, too. When he saw me he gave a loud, clear wailing wraaaah—*a spine-chilling call that is used to threaten a dangerous animal. To my right I saw a large black hand shaking a branch and bright eyes glaring threateningly through the foliage. Then came another savage* wraaaah *from behind. Up above, the big male began to sway the vegetation. I was surrounded.*

In her own words, here is Jane Goodall's compelling story of how she became one of the world's most famous naturalists.

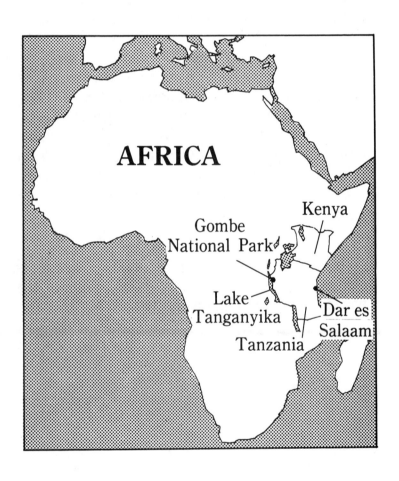

AFRICA

Kenya

Gombe
National Park

Lake
Tanganyika

Dar es
Salaam

Tanzania

My Life
With The Chimpanzees
by Jane Goodall

HOUGHTON MIFFLIN COMPANY

BOSTON

Atlanta   Dallas   Geneva, Illinois

Palo Alto   Princeton   Toronto

Special thanks to Pat MacDonald, Sue Engel,
Baron Hugo van Lawick, Neva Folk, and Robin Stevenson.

Book design by Alex Jay/Studio J
Mechanicals by Mary LeCleir
Typesetting by The Type Source

Editor: Ruth Ashby

"My Life" is a registered trademark of Byron Preiss Visual Publications, Inc.

CHAPTER 1

It was very stuffy and hot where I crouched, and the straw tickled my legs. There was hardly any light, either. But I could see the bird on her nest of straw. She was about five feet away from me, on the far side of the chicken house, and she had no idea I was there. If I moved I would spoil everything. So I stayed quite still. So did the chicken.

Presently, very slowly, she raised herself from the straw. She was facing away from me and bending forward. I saw a round white object gradually protruding from the feathers between her legs. It got bigger. Suddenly she gave a little wiggle and—plop!—it landed on the straw. I had actually watched the laying of an egg.

With loud, pleased clucks, the chicken shook her feathers, moved the egg with her beak, then proudly strutted her way out of the henhouse.

I tumbled out, stiff but excited, and ran all

1

the way to the house. My mother was just about to call the police. She had been searching for me for hours. She had no idea that I had been crouched all that time in the henhouse.

This was my first serious observation of animal behavior. I was five years old. How lucky it was that I had an understanding mother! Instead of being angry because I had given her a scare, she wanted to know all about the wonderful thing I had just seen.

Even though I was so young at the time, I can still remember a lot about that experience. I remember being puzzled about eggs. Where on a chicken was there an opening big enough for an egg to come out? I don't know if I asked anyone. If I did, no one told me. I decided to find out for myself. I remember thinking as I watched a hen going into one of the henhouses, "Ah, now I'll follow her and see what happens." And I remember how she rushed out, squawking in alarm, when I squeezed in after her. Obviously that was no good. I would have to get in first and wait until a hen decided to come in and lay her egg. That is why I was so long inside the henhouse. You have to be patient if you want to learn about animals.

When I grew up I became an ethologist—a long word that simply means a scientist who studies animal behavior. Most people, when they think of an animal, think of a creature with hair, such as a dog or a cat, a rabbit or a mouse, a horse or a cow. In fact, the word *animal* includes all living creatures except for plants. Jellyfish and insects, frogs and lizards, fish and birds are all animals just as cats and dogs are. But cats and dogs and horses are mammals, a special kind of animal. Humans are mammals, too.

You probably know all that. Children today know a lot more about these sorts of things than most adults did when I was your age. I remember having a huge argument with one of my aunts when I tried to make her believe that a whale was a mammal, not a fish. She wouldn't believe me and I cried. I was so frustrated.

The first person to be known as an ethologist was an Austrian, Konrad Lorenz. He is often called the Father of Ethology. He has always loved animals of all kinds. In addition to the dogs he keeps as pets, he has lived with all kinds of wild animals in his home near Vienna. Most of these animals have been perfectly free to come and go as they please.

Konrad Lorenz is best known for his work with greylag geese. He began raising and studying them in 1935. He still sometimes observes them even now, though he is over eighty years old.

Konrad Lorenz found that adult male and female geese are very faithful to each other. They fall in love, marry, and stay together until one of them dies. Then the one who is left does not marry again. If its mother is still alive, it goes back to her.

Konrad Lorenz has been "mother" to many geese—those he raised from the time they left their eggs. When they became adult, these geese left him and flew off with wild geese. But if they lost their mates, they came back to Lorenz.

He found that baby geese, when they hatch from their eggs, learn to follow the first moving object they see. Usually this is the mother goose. But when Lorenz raised geese, they followed him, instead! Then he discovered that if he hatched mallard duck eggs, the ducklings refused to follow him. But if they were hatched by a domestic duck, they followed her at once. What did the domestic duck do that he, Lorenz, didn't? She quacked. And her quacking sounded just like the quacking of a mallard duck. "Ah!" thought Lorenz, "that is the secret."

But scientists must always make tests. So, when the next lot of little ducklings hatched, Lorenz bent over them, quacked, and gradually moved away. They followed him! But it was very exhausting for him, taking his baby ducklings for a walk. If he stood up, towering high above them, or if he stopped quacking for more than a moment, they stopped following and began to cry loudly.

One day when Lorenz was walking the duck-

Konrad Lorenz with his ducks.
UPI/Bettmann Newsphotos.

lings, something made him look up. Peering over the tall wall around the meadow were some of the village people. They were staring in horror at the professor who, as far as they could see, was quacking away to himself while creeping along the ground in a most peculiar way. The ducklings were completely hidden in the long grass! No wonder the local people began to think the professor was crazy!

Ethologists are interested in how animals live their lives and why they behave the way they do. They are always asking questions. Why does a dog go round and round in a circle before it lies on its bed? How does a male moth find his female even if she is miles away? And so on.

Some ethologists go on and on asking questions about one particular kind of animal. Karl von Frisch, a German, was fascinated by honey-bees. How did a worker bee, returning to her hive after collecting honey, tell the other worker bees where to go? They could find her honey patch even if she, herself, didn't return. He found out that the returning bee performs a wonderful "waggle dance" that tells the others exactly where to go. She gives signals with her legs, her wings, and her tail. Then Frisch wanted to know whether she could see the beautiful colors of the flowers. How good was her sense of smell? The more answers he found, the more questions he asked.

Other ethologists are interested in a particular kind of behavior, such as the migration of birds. Or the different ways that juicy, nice-tasting insects mimic poisonous ones so they will not be eaten. Or the food-burying behavior of rats and mice. All ethologists ask questions. How? Why? What for?

Ethologists do their studying in different ways. Lorenz, as I said, took the animals he wanted to observe home with him. He had a very long-suffering wife!

Others, like Niko Tinbergen, another very famous early ethologist, do experiments out in the place where the animals live. Tinbergen is best known for his work with different kinds of sea gulls. He used to go out to the cliffs and rocky ledges where they breed. He spent a lot of time just watching them and writing down all the different things they did. But he also experimented. He learned some most extraordinary things. Some gulls, for example, become really excited if they see a giant egg. If Tinbergen placed such a monster near the nest of a herring gull or an oyster catcher, she would leave her own egg and desperately (and hopelessly) try to clamber onto the monstrous fake!

Then there are other ethologists who also go to the home of the animals they wish to study but do not do experiments. They just watch, wait for things to happen, and record what they hear and see. That is what I do. I began living among and studying the chimpanzees in Tanzania (it was Tanganyika when I began) in 1960. I am still studying them today, with the help of a Tanzanian field staff.

It took me a long time before I could get close enough to the chimps to make good observations. At first they were very shy. It took even longer before I understood their language of calls and gestures and the way they live in their society. But it was worth it. Because, apart from the human animal, the chimpanzee is the most fascinating animal of all. At least, that is what I think.

How on earth, you may wonder, did I get started? I will tell you.

CHAPTER 2

I was born in London, on April 3, 1934, but soon my parents moved to a house just outside the city. We lived there with Nanny, whom I adored, and a bull terrier called Peggy.

My father was an engineer with a job in London. His hobby was motor-racing. He drove a super, very expensive car, an Aston Martin. He sometimes took me for a ride in the car, but I don't remember much about that.

When I was five years old and my younger sister, Judy, was one, we all went to live in France. My parents wanted us to grow up speaking fluent French. But we had no time to learn—after only a few months, Hitler began the series of invasions that led to World War II. It was no longer safe for us to stay in France. Our house outside London had been sold, so we went to stay for a while in the lovely old manor house where my father had grown up.

The author at age 2. *The author with her mother, father, and sister Judy.*

The manor house was way out in the country, with a big farm next door. On the grounds were the ruins of a castle where the wicked king, Henry VIII, had shut up one of his wives. I remember those ruins: they seemed scary, all gray, crumbling stone and spider webs. There were bats in one room that still had part of its roof.

The manor house itself was very old, too. If you walked from one end to the other, you had to go down one or two steps here, up a little slope there, and so on, because different parts had been built at different times. It was made of gray stone, which was cool in summer and very cold in winter. There was no central heating. There were few places in England with central heating in those days. Inside the manor house there was always a faint smell from the oil lamps that were lit every evening—for there was no electricity. Even now, fifty years later, the smell of oil lamps always makes me think of the manor house.

I called my father's mother Danny Nutt. She loved geese, and there were always six or more grazing on the grass near the house. And there was a very big enclosure for the hens, with five henhouses in it, like the one in which I hid. I used to help feed the hens and collect the eggs. Finding them was rather like an Easter egg hunt, because many of the hens preferred to lay under bushes, rather than inside the henhouses.

There were cows in the fields nearby. In those days they were all milked by hand, and I loved to watch the dairymaid squirt the white milk into her pail while the cow placidly chewed its cud. There were some heavy farm horses grazing in the meadows and often a racehorse mare out to grass with her foal. Racehorses were the business of my father's brother, my uncle Rex. He had a small racing stable and managed a little racecourse about four miles from the manor house. Once, when I was two years old, I was allowed to ride on one of the racehorses. His name was Painstaker. Uncle Rex showed me how to make him move to the left or right by gently pulling one of the reins, and I managed to steer him, all by myself, in and out of the line of trees that ran along the main street of the little village. I can just remember that I was very proud.

As soon as England declared war on Germany, my father joined the army to help fight Hitler. Soon after that Nanny got married and went off to her own house with her husband. Then Mum, Judy, and I went to live with my other grandmother, Danny, in The Birches. The Birches is a lovely red brick house, with a big garden (that you would call a backyard) surrounded by a tall hedge that shuts out the world. It is in Bourne-

The Birches.

mouth, on the southern coast of England, just a few minutes walk from the sea of the English Channel. That is where I spent the rest of my childhood and my adolescence.

We shared The Birches with my mother's two sisters, Olwen (known as Olly) and Audrey. My uncle, a senior consultant surgeon in a huge London hospital, came home most weekends. During the war, all families with private houses that could were asked to take in people who temporarily found themselves without homes. And so we took in two single women for a while.

When America joined England in the fight against Hitler and the Nazis, many Yankee soldiers (as we called them) came over to England on their way to the fighting front in France, Holland, and Belgium. Some of them were stationed near us. Many of their tanks and trucks were parked along our quiet little road. The soldiers used to give us candy and other treats. We ourselves had very little food in England. Everything was rationed. We were allowed one egg apiece and two ounces of candy, and very little milk. The grown-ups usually gave us children most of their rations of candy, milk, and eggs. We needed coupons for everything, not just food. There were clothing coupons, gasoline coupons, and liquor coupons. And often, even if you *had* coupons, you couldn't get the things because they weren't available. Everything went to the soldiers, pilots, and sailors who were defending our island.

Some bombs fell on Bournemouth, though not many. We had an air-raid shelter installed in our house. It was a low, steel-roofed cage where the whole family would creep and wait, huddled together, from the time when we heard the air-raid warning until the welcome sound of the "All Clear."

However, for the most part we children were not much affected by the war. At the beginning we were too young to understand what was going on; by the end we had become used to news of battles, defeats, and victories.

During those war years I went to three different schools—a kindergarten and the equivalents of your junior and senior high schools. I never really liked any of them. I didn't mind the work—some of it I liked very much. But I hated having to leave home every morning, and I hated having to spend time indoors when I wanted to be outside. I longed for each day to end so that I could get home to my family. I longed for the weekends when I could go horseback riding. Most of all I longed for the holidays. Then, for days on end, I was free from school bells and school regimentation. On school days I hated to get up. Often Mum had to call me several times. On weekends and holidays it was different. Then I was always up

13

early, at least when the weather was good. I would go out onto the cliffs, with their pine trees and gorse bushes, or down to the beach.

I spent a lot of time in the garden. It was big and rather wild. There was one beech tree I loved so much that Danny gave it to me for my tenth birthday. My very own tree! I could climb high in its branches when I was happy. I'd sit and watch the birds and listen to their songs. Sometimes I took my homework up there. And I climbed it when I was sad, too, so I could be sad by myself. When I was sad I read a book. Mum taught me to do that. She said it would help me to forget my troubles, at least for a while. And afterward they might not seem so bad. I still do that today.

In the winter I loved to curl up in front of the fire and read. Our house was always filled with books, many of them from my mother's childhood. We couldn't afford many new books, but we belonged to the local library. One day for my weekend library book Mum brought me *The Story of Doctor Doolittle,* by Hugh Lofting. I read it all the way through. Then I read it through again. I had never before loved a book so much. I read it a third time before it had to go back—I finished it under the bedclothes with a flashlight after Mum had turned off the light. That was in November. And I shall never forget that Danny gave me the book for my very own that Christmas. I was

The author, Nanny and Judy.

seven years old. I think that was when I first decided I must go to Africa someday.

I read as many books as I could find about all sorts of animals, not only about those in Africa. I also loved stories of wolves, bears, and wolverines in North America and Canada, jaguars, anacondas and sloths in South America, orangutans, Indian elephants, and tapirs in Asia, and so on. I loved *The Jungle Book*, by Rudyard Kipling, with its tales of Mowgli, and especially

15

loved the books about Tarzan, by Edgar Rice Burroughs. But I never liked any of the Tarzan movies—my own imagined picture of Tarzan was more wonderful than any actor could possibly be.

Those animals seemed wonderful to me, but I knew that there was no way I could go and see them—not then. There was not even a zoo anywhere near us. And anyway, I wanted to watch *wild* animals, not animals in cages. So, as well as reading about those faraway animals, I also watched the wild creatures near my home—squirrels and birds and all kinds of insects. I started a nature club with four members—my sister and me and the Cary children, who came to stay almost every holiday. Sally was my age, Sue was Judy's age. I was the leader of the club—the Alligator Club—and chose to be Red Admiral. Sally was Puffin, Sue was Ladybird, and Judy was Trout.

In a hidden place in the garden, surrounded by bushes, we had our "camp," where we could light a little fire and boil water in a tin can, balanced on rocks. In an old trunk we kept four mugs, small supplies of tea and cocoa, and a spoon. Sometimes we had "feasts" there, with bits and pieces of food saved from meals. As it was wartime, we usually had nothing more than a few crusts of bread and an occasional biscuit. But it was fun—especially when we crept out into the garden at midnight, which we did partly because it was spooky and partly because it was strictly not allowed!

We went on lots of nature walks and wrote down what we saw—at least, I did. There were always books at home where I could look up the names of the different insects or birds we found.

Each of us owned two "racing" snails with numbers painted on their shells. We kept them in an old wooden box with no bottom and a piece of glass on the top. This meant that we could move their home to a new place in the garden each time they had finished eating the leaves growing inside. We also fed them lettuce leaves and other treats. We would line the snails up in a row and lay bets as to which would reach the end of a six-foot racetrack first. We used blades of grass to keep them in a straight line, but the blades had to be soft, and we could touch only the *side* of the snail's horn, not the sensitive end where the eye is located.

One summer we made a museum in the glass conservatory. We had a collection of pressed flowers and many shells, not only the local kinds from the Bournemouth beach but exotic ones collected by my adventurous great-grandfather during his travels to Australia and such places. Everything was very carefully labeled. Uncle Eric let us have a human skeleton leftover from his medical school days. That was our most prized exhibit.

Sally and I made Judy and Sue—we called them The Little Ones—go out into the street and ask passersby to come and see the museum. Afterward we asked them to make a contribution to a society for the protection of old horses—they were rescued from the butcher and put out to graze at Cherry Tree Farm.

When the Carys went back home at the end of the holidays, I used to put together an Alligator Club magazine. It was filled with nature notes, drawings of insect anatomy, and other such things. The other members were supposed to contribute, and make comments and suggestions—but they hardly ever did.

Every Saturday during term time, and at least twice a week over the holidays, I went to a riding school in the country. We couldn't afford to pay for riding lessons every week, but that didn't matter. I just loved to be there, to be near the horses and ponies, to learn how to look after them. The only part I didn't much enjoy was the endless cleaning of the tack—the saddles and bridles. Every single day they had to be washed, then rubbed with saddle soap. Miss Bush, who owned the riding stable, was really strict about cleaning the tack, and we had to do it even after the longest days.

I was happiest when I was invited, during the holidays, to stay with Poosh, Miss Bush's assistant. We would get up before it was light and go down to the warm kitchen where Poosh's mother, a comfortable Scotswoman, was already beginning work on breakfast. We drank hot tea and munched digestive biscuits. Then we went out into the first light of dawn to catch the ponies from the fields where they grazed during the night. We rode them, bareback with just a halter, to the riding stable. Often I had as many as five ponies, one on each side of me and two behind, on a long rope. Then I would groom them, give each of them a pile of hay, and get the tack ready for the first ride.

Eventually I was trusted to take clients out for rides. I got lots of free riding that way. And when I was fourteen I used to ride Poosh's horse, Quince, in horse shows. On those days I had the thrill of getting up even earlier, grooming Quince until she shone, plaiting her mane and tail, oiling her hooves, then traveling with her in the horse trailer. I don't think we ever won anything, but we sometimes came third or fourth in the jumping. And it was always exciting.

Once I went fox hunting. I'd never thought about what that really meant before. I'd just imagined the excitement of jumping great hedges, the challenge of trying to keep up with the best riders, and the thrilling sound of the hunting horn. I hadn't thought about the fox.

I kept up only too well. So I saw the fox dug up out of his den, where he had at last found safety (he thought), and I watched the huntsman throw the exhausted creature to the hounds to be torn up. Then I felt sick, and the excitement of the hunt was gone. I never went hunting again.

Most of all, when I think of my childhood, I think of Rusty. There will never again be a dog like Rusty in my life. He wasn't even our dog—he lived in a hotel around the corner. I met him at a time when I used to take out a most beautiful collie called Budleigh for a lady who owned a sweetshop. I knew that she couldn't give him as much exercise as he needed, so I used to run down to the beach with him almost every day. Rusty began to tag along.

I used to try to teach "Buds" a few tricks—such as sitting up and begging for a tidbit, or sitting with a biscuit on his nose until I said "Okay." Then he could lower his nose and eat the biscuit as it fell to the ground. I never tried to teach Rusty anything. Then, one day when I was trying to teach Buds to shake hands, Rusty suddenly held out his paw. Of course, I made a big fuss over him—I had never thought him very intelligent before. But after that I began to teach *him*. In only three lessons he learned the biscuit-

Rusty.

on-the-nose trick—but instead of lowering his nose when I said "Okay," he gave a little upward jerk of his head so that the reward was tossed into the air. He caught and ate it as it fell.

Rusty learned everything I tried to teach him. He would lie down and "die" on command and wait, even if I went out of sight for more than ten minutes. I discovered he could climb a tall workman's ladder—at first I found him following me as I climbed, but later he would go up without me if I asked him to. He would jump anything—even through a hoop. I never punished him if he

21

did something wrong, but I made a great fuss over him if he did it right. And that was enough encouragement for him—I hardly ever rewarded him with food. In fact, I almost never gave him any food, ever. He still slept at the hotel. But as soon as he was let out in the morning—about six-thirty—he came and barked at our front door. He trotted back for his evening meal, then returned to us until it was bedtime. We asked the owners if they minded. They didn't care at all.

There was one way in which Rusty was different from most dogs. He loved to be dressed up. Most dogs hate to be dressed up, and it is very unkind of you to try to force it on them. But when I put clothes on Rusty, he went all floppy, like a rag doll. Sometimes I put him in pajamas and wheeled him around the streets in our old pram. But it was very important not to laugh at him. He hated that and would walk off at once, trailing clothes behind him.

Rusty taught me so much about animal be-havior, lessons I have remembered all my life. He taught me that dogs can think things out—that they can reason. If, for example, I threw a ball from an upstairs window, he would watch where it landed, then bark for the door to be opened, rush downstairs, bark for an outside door to be opened, then go and find the ball. He could plan, too. When it was very hot he sometimes took himself off

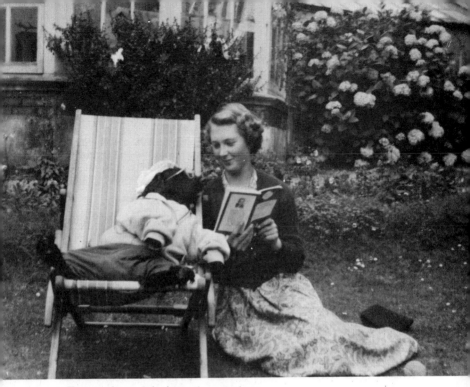

Rusty loved being dressed up.

along the street to the sea, had a swim, then trotted back, wet and cool.

Rusty was the only dog I have ever known who seemed to have a sense of justice. If he did something he *knew* was wrong (that is, something I had taught him was wrong), then he apologized the way dogs do, by rolling over on his back and grinning. But if I was cross about something that *he* thought was okay, then he sulked.

For example, I had taught him to "shut the door": He would jump up and bang it shut. One day he did this with very wet, muddy paws, and *without* my having asked him (he wanted attention). "Oh Rusty—bad dog!" I said. He stared at me, then went and sat facing a wall, his nose a couple of inches away, and stayed that way even when I said "walkies!" Not until I knelt down and apologized did he move from his place and, gradually, become friendly again. He behaved like this on four quite separate occasions.

Another reason why I hated the end of the holidays was that I had to leave Rusty every morning when I went off to school.

At school I always did fairly well, especially in the subjects I found interesting, such as English, History, Scripture, and, of course, Biology. Math and languages I found more difficult, so I had to work harder at them. I usually came second or third in the end of term overall results. One very brainy girl (my high school was for girls only) always came first. My best friend, Marie-Claude Mange, known as Clo, was either second, just above me, or third, just below me. For my last two years I took a strange mixture of subjects— Biology, English, and History. As they were the ones I had always liked best, those last years were my happiest at school.

I got good marks during my final exams when I was eighteen. And then, quite suddenly, my school days were over. What would I do next? I only wanted to watch and write about animals. How could I get started? How could I make a living doing that?

CHAPTER 3

The first thing I did when I left school was to go and spend four months with a family in Germany. After the war my mother felt that I ought to visit the country that had been our enemy. She thought it was important that I should realize that though Hitler and the Nazis were evil, there were also ordinary Germans who did not like Hitler.

But I didn't enjoy that visit much. The part of Germany I was in was bleak, flat, and dreary. I remember best going with the younger daughter, Helga, to visit the neighboring farms, eating thick, dark bread in farmhouse kitchens, and learning to wear clogs. And I remember early morning walks through flat, frosty fields where I saw hares bound away over the white, hard ground.

I was supposed to learn German. But the family was so keen to learn good English that they hardly ever spoke German to me. Because, as

I've told you, I was bad at languages, I only picked up a smattering.

One thing I have never forgotten. I went on a visit to the city of Cologne. Like so many other German cities, it had been heavily bombed by Allied forces during the war. As you looked out across the flattened, battered city, you could see the spire of Cologne Cathedral. It rose, quite undamaged, from the rubble of the surrounding buildings. To me it seemed like a message from God, telling us that however bad things may seem, in the end, goodness will win. All my childhood I had been to church. Not every Sunday, but many Sundays. Seeing the spire of Cologne Cathedral that day meant more to me than all the sermons I had ever listened to.

When I got back from Germany I went to a secretarial school in London. Mum said that secretaries could get jobs anywhere in the world. And so I learned how to type and do shorthand and simple bookkeeping.

I loved being in London visiting art galleries and going to concerts. I never learned to play a musical instrument, but I loved to listen to classical music. Of course, as I still had little money, I walked everywhere and sat in the very cheapest seats.

I got to know a lot of people. Young men sometimes took me out to dinner or to a theater. I had never had time for boys before; I had been far too busy with horses and walking in the country and Rusty. But now I had left school and was out in the big world.

When I had my secretary's diploma, I went home for a while and got a job at Olly's clinic. Olly was a physiotherapist to the children in the whole of the Bournemouth region, and she ran a clinic. Several times a week different doctors came in to examine their patients. I was there to type their letters.

Olly's patients had all kinds of problems. There were tiny babies with club feet, children who had paralyzed limbs from polio, adolescents dying from muscular dystrophy. Some of the children couldn't walk and would have to spend the rest of their lives in wheelchairs. Some could move about, but only by wearing clumsy leg-irons or crutches. There were children who would never be able to look after themselves. There was a little boy who was an "athetoid." This is caused by damage to the brain stem during birth. The poor victims cannot properly control their muscles. Their arms and legs jerk violently. So do their faces when they try to speak. Usually it is very difficult to understand what they are trying to say.

Olly told me a wonderful story. In the old days, people thought that athetoids were crazy.

Often they were put in mental institutions. Well, there was a little athetoid girl whose parents were rich. They didn't want her shut into one of those places for the insane, so they paid for her to stay in the children's ward of a big hospital. No one spent much time with her. One day a famous doctor was in the ward. He told a rather adult joke. None of the children laughed—they didn't understand it. But suddenly the doctor saw the eyes of the "crazy" girl—they were sparkling with fun. He knew that *she* had understood. He was amazed. He took her home with him and gave her special lessons. She was so intelligent that she not only learned to talk but soon passed all her school exams. Now we know that athetoids are almost always unusually bright.

I learned so much at that clinic. Ever since then, when things have gone wrong in my life, I remember how lucky I am to be healthy. I thank God for that, and I feel more determined to solve my problems or get over my sadness, or whatever. And I feel a special closeness with people who are crippled or disabled in any way.

After working at the clinic for six months, I got a job in Oxford. I had thought of going to the famous university there, but Mum could not afford to send me unless I won a major scholarship. For a major scholarship I needed a language. And, as you know, I didn't have one. Well, I thought, a job there is the next best thing. The job itself was very boring—I worked in the filing department of the administrative building of the university. But I lived in a "bed sit" in a house with some Oxford graduate students—and so I got to know many other students. I had lots of fun—it was almost like being a student myself, without the work!

What I liked best, though, was the river. I used to take out a canoe and paddle silently along, early in the morning or late in the evening. I saw water birds, moorhens, kingfishers, and swans. The swans were a bit scary, especially when they had a nest or babies, because then they are sometimes aggressive. I knew one man who once had his leg broken when an angry swan, thinking he was after one of her babies, attacked him.

I also learned to punt, which is much harder than canoeing. You push along a flat-bottomed boat with a long pole, hoisting it, hand over hand, out of the water, then pushing it down hard and driving the boat forward. There are two problems. One is trying to keep the punt straight. The other is pushing the pole too hard into a patch of mud at the bottom of the river. Often you see a beginner either leaving his pole behind, or clinging on so desperately that he is pulled from the punt and splashes into the water. I very often got a ducking when I was learning!

The author and her father, Mortimer Goodall. She is wearing her dress for the May ball.

I went to a couple of the famous May balls at Oxford. My first ball gown was white net, with pale gray swan feathers scattered over it, each one kept in place with a sequin. It was very expensive originally, but had been worn by a model in a fashion show, so I got it very cheap, indeed. I felt like a princess when I wore that gown.

I remember one other dress—a wonderful crimson red lace. I am sure my mother did without cinemas and all sorts of other things in order to buy it for me. It had to be a good dress, for Uncle Michael and Auntie Joan were going to present me to Queen Elizabeth in Buckingham Palace. First I had to learn a full state curtsy. I had lessons from a funny old lady. She told me to practice and practice, always balancing something on my head. So I was quite proficient by the time I curtsied to the queen and Prince Philip. It was a magnificent occasion.

After a year at Oxford, I went back to London and an absolutely fascinating job. I worked at a film studio that made documentary films. They specialized in medical films but also made some about motor racing, and others that were just advertisements. My actual job was to choose the music for the film. I also learned how to edit, how to make sound tracks, how to mix, and all sorts of other things about filmmaking.

I lived in my father's flat. By then my parents had divorced, but they were still good friends. And it was nice that I got to know my father a bit better during that year when I was in London.

What about my dream of Africa? Had I forgotten it? Absolutely not. I spent hours wandering about in the Natural History Museum. I continued to read books about animals, especially African animals. And, even while I loved my job, I knew that it was just filling in time. Always I was waiting for my lucky break.

When that lucky break finally came, I was ready. It happened one Wednesday morning. I received a letter from my school friend, Clo. I'd almost forgotten about her; we'd lost touch over the previous few years. And now, out of the blue, she invited me to go and visit her in Kenya, where her parents had just bought a farm. Kenya, Africa! You bet I would go!

First I had to earn the money. Wonderful though my film studio job was, I was paid a very small salary. I gave my notice and went back home. There I got a job as a waitress. I worked in a big, old-fashioned hotel just around the corner from The Birches.

Perhaps you think it's easy to be a waitress —or a waiter? I did. I quickly learned how wrong I was. There were so many skills I had to master in order to become a good waitress. I learned to deftly lift a slice of meat or a helping of vegetables with serving spoon and fork neatly manipulated in one hand while holding the dish with the other. I got especially skillful at carrying several plates at the same time, without a tray. My record was thirteen plates with little servings of fish on each!

Each weekend I put my wages and my tips under the carpet in the drawing room. One evening, when I had been working for four months, the family gathered around, we drew the curtains (so no one could look in), and counted my earnings. How exciting—I now had enough money, along with the small amount I had saved while in London, for a round-trip fare to Africa!

CHAPTER 4

My first journey to Africa was by sea on a passenger liner, the *Kenya Castle*. I was twenty-three years old. I shall remember that wonderful voyage as long as I live.

We sailed right down the west coast of Africa, calling in at the Canary Isles (of course I thought of Doctor Doolittle's adventures there with the pirates, though nothing so exciting happened to me). Then we rounded the Cape of Good Hope, called in at Cape Town and Durban, and finally Beira. I wanted the trip to go on forever. I loved being up on deck, where I watched the sea and glimpsed dolphins, sharks, and flying fish. I especially loved it when it was rough and most passengers were in their cabins. I was lucky. I never felt seasick.

The South African towns of Cape Town and Durban were very beautiful. But I hated the practice of apartheid—the legal separation of

33

blacks and whites. It was awful to see seats at a bus stop marked "Slegs Blancs"—Afrikaans for "Whites Only." The same signs were on the bathing beaches, the restaurants—almost everywhere.

Twenty-one days after leaving London we steamed into Mombasa, the coastal port of Kenya. I had arrived. I had no idea what lay ahead, but I knew it would be exciting.

I went by train to Nairobi, the capital city of Kenya. It was a two-day train ride, so I got to see some of the countryside and, even from a distance, some wild animals. But none of it seemed real then—it was like seeing a movie landscape.

In Nairobi I was met by Clo. On our way to her farm I saw my first giraffe close up. He stood on his long legs in the middle of the dirt road, his long neck towering above the car, and looked down his long nose at us. His beautiful dark eyes were fringed with long lashes. He was chewing acacia thorns, and I could see that his long tongue was almost black. Finally he turned and cantered away. It looked as though he ran in slow motion. When I saw him, that amazing long, long animal, I finally knew, for sure, that I was really there. I had actually gotten to the Africa of my dreams—the Africa of Doctor Doolittle and Tarzan.

I spent three wonderful weeks on Clo's farm in

a part of Kenya called the Kinankop, or White Highlands. Then I had to move to Nairobi to start my temporary job. I've always felt it is an unforgivable thing to dump yourself on friends and then just stay on and on, sponging on their hospitality. So when I was still in England, we had arranged for my job with a big company that had a branch in Kenya. It was very boring, but I could earn my own money and be independent while I tried to find a way to work somehow with animals.

After two months I met the man who made all my dreams come true. "If you are interested in animals," someone told me, "you must meet Louis Leakey." Leakey was an anthropologist and paleontologist who was interested in animals and Early Man. So I made an appointment and went to see him in his big, untidy office, strewn with papers, fossil bones, teeth, stone tools, and all kinds of other things—including a big cage in which lived a minute mouse with her six babies.

Louis offered me a job immediately—his secretary had just given her notice. What amazing luck! I think he would have found work for me anyway, because he was impressed by how much I knew about African animals.

Louis took me around Nairobi National Park. Being with him was a wonderful experience. He had all kinds of fascinating stories about animals he'd seen during his years of living in Kenya. He knew perhaps more than any white man about the Kikuyu, too, since his missionary father had allowed him to grow up almost as part of the tribe. When he was two days old he was set outside the house in his crib, and in accordance with Kikuyu custom, all the elders of the tribe walked past to give him their blessing. To do this each of them spat on him! Later, as an adolescent, he went through the initiation rights with the other Kikuyu boys with whom he had grown up.

Before I started to work in the museum, Louis and his wife Mary took Gillian, another girl who worked at the museum, and me on an expedition. We went to Olduvai Gorge in Tanganyika.

That was one of the most exciting adventures in my life. In 1957, Olduvai Gorge, which is now famous, was known to very few white people. There was no road leading there—not even a track. When we left the trail from Ngorongoro Crater to Seronera (a trail that is now a well-marked road across the Serengeti plains), Gillian and I had to sit up on the roof of the over-loaded Land Rover to look for the faint tire marks left by the Leakeys the year before. They had been going for three or four months every summer to look for fossils. They already knew a great deal about the prehistoric creatures that roamed the Serengeti in bygone years. They knew that apelike men had lived there, too. They had found many of their simple stone tools but, at that time, none of their bones had been discovered.

After a long journey, during which we had stopped twice to set up camp, we arrived at the gorge. There, under some shady acacia trees, we set up the tents that would be home for the next three months. Presently the big truck arrived, loaded with more equipment and the African field staff who would help with the digging.

It was nearly dark by the time they had their tents up. Louis and Mary slept in the truck, once it was empty. They put their two beds into it and a few boxes to use as tables and storage compartments. The truck became a sort of camper.

As we sat around our campfire that evening, eating a scratch meal from tins, I heard the distant, grunting roar of a lion. And later, as I lay on my little cot, I heard a strange, high-pitched sound that I later learned was the "giggling" of hyenas squabbling over some prey.

I had never been so happy. There I was, far, far from any human dwellings, out in the wilds of Africa, with animals all around me in the night. Wild, free animals. That was what I had dreamed of all my life.

Digging for fossils under the hot tropical sun was very hard work. The African team prepared the site by using picks and shovels to remove the

The author at Olduvai Gorge. Louis Leakey is standing on the left.

topsoil. Once they got down near the layer of fossils that Louis and Mary wanted to work on, Mary insisted on doing the last of the heavy work herself. If an important fossil got broken by a pick, it was better that she should do it than one of the Africans. I was strong and very healthy, and I offered to help her. We got on well together, sweating away as we swung the heavy implements.

Once we were down to the fossil "bed" we chipped away at the hard soil with hunting knives, searching for bones. Once we found a bone, we used dental picks (the same kind dentists use in your mouth) to carefully free the precious relic from its resting place. The final cleaning was done back in Nairobi.

I always remember the first time I held in my hand the bone of a creature that had walked the earth millions of years before. I had dug it up myself. A feeling of awe crept over me. I thought, "Once this creature stood here. It was alive, had flesh and hair. It had its own smell. It could feel hunger and thirst and pain. It could enjoy the early morning sun."

In the afternoon we all gathered for an hour under a grass roof whose walls were criss-crossed poles. There we sorted through our morning finds. We gave each one a number, then stored it carefully away.

Two years later the Leakeys found the skull of an apelike creature who became known as Dear Boy or George. He was also called the Nutcracker Man because he had such large teeth and thick, strong jaws. His official name is *Australopithecus robustus*.

Before his skull was dug up, no remains of any humanlike creature had been discovered at Olduvai, although people searching there had found plenty of evidence to show that such creatures had lived there long, long ago. I myself had found ancient stone tools, very crude and primitive, that had probably been used as hammers. Dear Boy, at last, gave Louis and Mary some idea of what the hammer-wielder must have looked like.

I am so glad that I knew Olduvai before that famous discovery. It was so wild and so remote when I was there. Every day, after work was finished, Gillian and I were allowed to wander off on our own. Once we almost bumped into a black rhino. Rhinos are very shortsighted, and he knew something was wrong. He snorted and pawed the ground before turning and trotting off, tail held high in the air.

Another time I had a sort of prickly feeling in my back. I turned around and there was a young male lion, about ninety feet away, gazing at Gillian and me with much interest. "We must walk calmly across the gorge and climb up onto the plain," I told Gillian. She, however, wanted to hide away from the lion in the thick undergrowth at the bottom of the gorge. In the end we did what I wanted. The lion followed for about three hundred feet, then stood and watched as we climbed up into the open. Later, Louis told me we had done the right thing.

I hated leaving when the three months were up. We all did. My only consolation was that I could continue to work for Louis and to learn about animals.

I quickly settled down to my new job when we got back to Nairobi. Not only did I work all day at a desk in Louis's cluttered office, but I moved into one of the museum staff flats. There I could be with a group of people who were all really knowledgeable about African mammals, birds, reptiles, and insects. What a lot I learned during those days!

My friend Sally came out from England to share the flat with me. She had become a teacher, and she taught five- to six-year-old children at a nearby school.

It was not long before we had a collection of animals. People kept bringing them to me: animals who had been orphaned and needed a home, animals who had been rescued from African markets. First came a bush baby, Levi.

A bush baby, or galago, is a small, squirrel-like animal related to a monkey. Bush babies have huge ears, large, round eyes, and long, bushy tails. They make a loud wailing sound at night that, to some people, sounds like the crying of babies. There are several different species—Levi was one of the smaller varieties.

In the daytime he was mostly asleep in a large gourd on top of a cupboard in Louis's office. Sometimes, if Louis had a visitor, Levi woke up when he heard the strange voice. He would peer sleepily out of the gourd, gaze down, and then take a flying leap and land on the newcomer's shoulders. One

*Levi, the
bush baby.*

man, I'm sure, almost had a heart attack from fright! Louis never minded—he said that people in Africa should always be prepared for anything to happen! In the evening Levi leapt around the room catching insects attracted to the lights. He also ate a lot of fruit and mealworms. I often left the door open, but he never went away—though he sometimes visited the other residents of the museum flats and startled them as he leapt through door or window in pursuit of some insect.

I next acquired a vervet monkey, Kobi, and a dwarf mongoose, Kip. Both were tied onto stalls at a local market. They became very fond of each other, and Kobi often sat holding Kip in his arms.

Then came a wife for Kobi, named Lettuce, and a wife for Kip, known simply as Mrs. Kip. Somehow we got a hedgehog, and Sally contributed a white and black rat, rescued from the school lab during vacation.

There were some more conventional pets, too: Tana, a beautiful white and lemon cocker spaniel who was given to me, and Hobo, a springer spaniel I looked after for a friend. There was also a Siamese cat, Nanky-Poo.

As often as possible Sally and I would get into my old car, call all the animals, and drive out to the Langata Forest, near where Louis Leakey and his family lived. I would open the car door and all the animals would tumble out—except Nanky-Poo, who stayed in the car, and the rat and the hedgehog, who stayed at home. But the moment I started the engine, they all came running back.

I always hoped my monkeys would wander off to live in the forest, but they never did. Once an animal has been caught and tamed, it is very hard for it to go back to the wild. Only two of our animals did—the hedgehog, whom I freed when it was fully grown, and Mrs. Kip. Kip himself refused to leave. In fact I had him the longest of all my animals, for he came back to England with me and lived in Bournemouth for many years, with the run of house and garden.

It is almost never a good thing to keep wild

43

animals as pets. They are adapted to live in the wild. They can't cope with human ways as our dogs and cats can. And almost always they come to sad ends. Kip, I'm afraid, got out into the street on a cold November night and simply vanished. He must have died so miserable and cold. Danny, who adored him, and who had accidentally let him out, almost died too—she went off searching for him and stayed out for hours. We found her blue and shivering with cold. She had to be given brandy and put to bed. She was well over eighty at the time.

Of course, even cats and dogs can come to tragic ends. It was not long after I had met Louis Leakey that he took me with him to search for the body of an Irish wolfhound who, her owner said, had been taken by a leopard the night before. Louis, skilled in bush lore, followed the leopard's tracks and the trail of dried blood, until we found the body of the huge dog. It had been dragged some way up a tree. We knew that the leopard, who had not eaten very much, was somewhere nearby. The hair stood up on the back of my neck as I vainly looked among the branches and into the tangled undergrowth all around.

Louis had earlier organized a plan to capture leopards who made trouble around people's homes and release them in one of the national parks.

He directed a truck to bring a big, live trap to within about three hundred feet of the dead hound, which was then dragged across the ground and put into the trap. Louis hoped the leopard would follow the trail, enter the trap, and thus be captured. The plan worked perfectly. The next morning Louis took me to watch as the leopard, in his trap, was loaded into the truck for the long drive to his new hunting grounds. He was so beautiful, so terrified, so defiantly brave as he spat and snarled at his human captors through the bars. I hope he made it in his new home. But leopards are territorial, and he would have had to battle with at least one other male before he could carve out a home range for himself.

When I'd been working at the museum for nine months, I had saved up enough money to give Mum a surprise—I sent her a check that would pay for her to visit me. All my life, up to that time, she had been doing things for me. Now, at last, I could do something for her.

She came out by plane. She loved Africa, as I had known she would. She loved meeting all my human and animal friends. Very quickly she made many friends of her own and was invited all over the place. She got to see a lot of Kenya during the short time she was there.

We talked about my future. Louis never minded if his scientific staff had higher degrees or not:

45

The important thing, as far as he was concerned, was that they had knowledge and were hard-working and dedicated. So I could have gone on at the museum. Or I could have learned a whole lot more about fossils and become a paleontologist.

But both those careers had to do with *dead* animals. And I still wanted to work with *living* animals. My childhood dream was as strong as ever: Somehow I must find a way to watch free, wild animals living their own, undisturbed lives. I wanted to learn things that no one else knew, uncover secrets through patient observation. I wanted to come as close to talking to animals as I could, to be like Doctor Doolittle. I wanted to move among them without fear, like Tarzan.

From time to time, ever since we'd come back from Olduvai, Louis had talked about some chimpanzees living on the shores of a far-off lake in Tanganyika. They were much stronger than men, he said. It might be dangerous to study them. It would certainly be difficult. But he was anxious to find out about their lives. Perhaps, he thought, knowing how they lived would help him to understand more about the way our own Stone Age ancestors lived. For chimpanzees and humans are biologically very closely related, indeed.

Because I had no training, no degree, no experience, I had not imagined that I could be chosen for such a study. But of course, I desper-

The author and Louis Leakey.

ately wanted to try. One day I told Louis so.

"I've been waiting for you to tell me that," he said, his eyes twinkling. "Why did you think I talked about those chimpanzees to you?" He told me that it didn't matter about my lack of experience or my lack of a degree. He wanted to send someone who had a mind "uncluttered by theories," someone who would watch carefully and record accurately. He preferred someone who truly wanted to live among the apes and learn about their behavior to someone who simply wanted an academic degree. Above all, he said, he needed someone who had endless patience.

Obviously, I was that person! This was what I had been so long waiting for, the kind of thing I had come to Africa hoping to do. Louis warned me that it would be a long and difficult task. He told me that if I succeeded, I would have to go to a university and get a degree. And he told me that before I could begin, he would have to try to find the money I would need.

We decided it would be best if I went back to England to learn all I could about chimpanzees while he tried to raise the money. Mum and I went back together on a boat, through the Suez Canal, calling at Aden and Barcelona. So when I got back to London, a year after setting out, I had been all around the African continent.

CHAPTER 5

It was a whole year from the time when I left Africa to the time when I actually arrived among the chimpanzees. Sometimes, as month followed month, I felt sure I would never get there. Surely, I told myself, it's all too good to be true.

Once I got back to England I got a job at the London Zoo. I didn't work directly with the animals, but I helped in the television film library there. At the same time I spent hours watching the chimpanzees. There was a beautiful male, called Dick, and two females. But Dick had been shut up in a small cage for so long that he was almost mad. He would sit in a corner and seem to be counting his fingers while his mouth opened and shut, opened and shut. I made a vow to myself that one day I would try to help chimps in zoos to have a better life.

I read everything I could about chimps, but almost all of it was about chimps in labs or in

London Zoo. Dick counting his fingers.

people's homes. Only one man had tried to watch them in the wild. He had done this for only two and a half months and had not learned much. But the more I read the more I realized how intelligent chimpanzees really are. Everyone agreed that they are more like human beings than any other creature alive today. How lucky I was, I thought, to be going to study them for months and months in their own forest home.

At last Louis wrote to say that he had managed to get enough money for me to begin my study. He had also managed to get the British government official in Tanganyika (which is now Tanzania, after its merger with Zanzibar) to agree that I could work in the Gombe Stream Game Reserve. In 1960, Tanganyika was still under British colonial rule, and Louis said it had been very difficult to get this permission. In those days it was not thought at all safe for a young, single girl to go into the wilds of Africa and study animals. In fact, Louis was told that I would not be allowed to go by myself. I had to choose a companion.

Well, I chose Mum. She was thrilled to come. She had loved Africa and was longing to go back. She also wanted to help me get started in my new venture. She would not be able to stay much longer than three or four months, but we hoped that the authorities would get used to me during this time and let me stay on alone.

With great excitement we packed and flew out to Nairobi. Louis met us and took us to a hotel where we would stay while everything was prepared for the expedition.

What a lot we had to get ready! All our camping gear—tent, bedding, cooking things. Cans of food. Drab clothes for me so I would blend in with the greens and browns of the forest. Binoculars. And lots of notebooks and paper for writing up my notes.

Then came a terrible disappointment. Louis had received a long telegram from the head of the

Game Department in Tanganyika. He informed us that there were fishermen who were fighting over who should fish from which beach along the lake shore of the Game Reserve. It was not safe for Miss Goodall and her mother. We must delay our safari.

Louis knew how disappointed I was. He arranged for Mum and me to use his little motor-boat on Lake Victoria, in Kenya. We would be taken to an uninhabited island, Lolue, where I could watch vervet monkeys. It would be good practice and would give me some experience in how to approach and observe wild monkeys.

After a train ride, we settled into the lovely little boat and set off on the trip to Lolue Island. The captain was a wonderful African, Hassan. He was helped by the much younger Hamisi.

I loved watching those monkeys. It took only about ten days before I could get quite close to the troop I chose to watch.

The island, which was about nine square miles, had a thick belt of quite dense bush around the edge. The middle was grass covered, with a few low trees and some big rocks. Mostly I stayed in the grassy part and watched the monkeys as they moved about in the trees and low bushes. When it was hot in the middle of the day, they moved deeper into the forest belt, toward the lake. One day, when I had been there nearly two weeks and the monkeys were quite used to me, I decided to try to follow them into the forest to see what they did.

I was going slowly along one of the tunnels made by hippos, through the thick undergrowth where they move inland to graze at night, when I heard something moving toward me. Hoping it wasn't a hippo, I crept into the bushes. Hippos can be dangerous, especially when frightened. There was no breeze in the dense vegetation. My scent would hang heavily in the air and betray my presence to any animal nearby.

When I finally saw what was approaching, my heart gave a great thump. It was much more frightening than any hippo. It was an African, dressed only in a loincloth, with a spear in one hand. I knew at once that he was one of the crocodile poachers that Hassan had told me about. And I knew that he could not fail to see me as he passed.

So I stepped out into the hippo tunnel and said, "Jambo"—"How are you?" The man stopped as if I had hit him and, quick as lightning, raised his arm. The tip of the spear was pointed directly toward me. He seemed ready to impale me. But suddenly, perhaps because he saw I was just a white girl, he lowered his spear. I began to breathe again! He was very angry. He shouted at me. I couldn't understand all he said, but I did

53

gather that he would kill me if he saw me there again!—and that I should leave the island as quickly as possible. Finally, he went away.

I didn't feel like watching monkeys anymore that day. I went to the edge of the lake and signaled for Hassan to come and fetch me. When Hassan heard what had happened, he was very angry. He immediately rowed around the island to the poachers' camp and talked to them. Finally they said they would leave me alone if I kept to my part of the island and never went near their camp. I was ready enough to stick to this arrangement. But I never really trusted them, and whenever I went after the monkeys along the dimly lit hippo tunnels, I was always expecting to see a sinister human shape lurking there.

After nearly four weeks I had learned quite a lot about the monkeys. Then, when Hassan came to fetch me one evening, he told me that a message had come through on the radio with the news that I could now go to Gombe. I went back to the island one more day—I felt I had to take my leave of the little monkeys I had come to love—Pierre and Maggie and Lucy and her little baby Grock, who had been born a few days before. And then, early the next morning, we set off back to the mainland.

Everything was ready for us to go, once we got back to Nairobi. The botanist from the museum, Bernard Verdcout, was driving Mum and me to

Kigoma, the nearest town to Gombe and the chimps. Once we had loaded everything into his Land Rover, it was so full I was surprised it moved at all!

The journey took three days. Much of the drive was through woodland infested with tsetse flies. When we stopped during the day the flies, which had been following the car, dived down on us in search of blood. They are ugly gray insects, with such quick flight that they are hard to kill. Their bites are painful. In some areas they can give you sleeping sickness.

At last we reached Kigoma. We checked in at the little hotel, washed, and then went to visit the regional commissioner, the head of government there. We had simply gone to introduce ourselves. But after greeting us the commissioner looked serious. "I'm sorry. I can't allow you to go on to Gombe now," he said. "There has been a terrible rebellion among the Africans across the lake in the Belgian Congo. They are killing many white people. We don't know how the Tanganyika Africans will react—they might also decide to rebel. Until we know, you must stay in Kigoma."

Would I ever get to study the chimpanzees?

We went back to the hotel. We soon found that Kigoma was filled with refugees from the Congo (now known as Zaire). Many of them had seen family or friends killed and had rushed away, leaving everything behind them. Some of them were wounded. It was a sad and depressing time.

Most of the refugees were being looked after in a huge Belgian-owned building close to the lake shore. All the people living in Kigoma got together to help.

Two days later more refugees arrived. Luckily, by then many of the first arrivals had left Kigoma. Even so, things were getting crowded. Mum, Bernard, and I all moved into one room so that a few extra homeless people could stay in the hotel. Soon after that, we moved out of the hotel altogether. We camped near the lake and felt a bit better. The Kigoma people were very kind and invited us in for meals and baths.

At long last the British authorities decided it was safe for us to go to Gombe. Bernard stayed until we had stowed all our gear on the government launch that would take us along the lake. Bernard told me later that he thought he might never see us again—he thought we were crazy, that the plan to study the chimps was highly dangerous. Afterward I learned that many other people had thought the same as Bernard. Luckily, Louis had not listened to any of them!

The launch cast off and began chugging northward along the lake shore. Finally we were on the last stage of the long journey from England, via Lake Victoria, to Chimpanzee Land!

CHAPTER 6

July 16, 1960, was a day I shall remember all my life. It was when I first set foot on the shingle and sand beach of Chimpanzee Land—that is, Gombe National Park. I was twenty-six years old.

Mum and I were greeted by the two African game scouts who were responsible for protecting the thirty square miles of the park. They helped us to find a place where we could put up our old ex-army tent.

We chose a lovely spot under some shady trees near the small, fast-flowing Kakombe Stream. In Kigoma (before setting out), we had found a cook, Dominic. He put up his little tent some distance from ours and quite near the lake.

When camp was ready I set off to explore. It was already late afternoon, so I could not go far. There had been a grass fire not long before, so all the vegetation of the more open ridges and peaks had burned away. This made it quite easy to move

The author and her mother, Vanne Goodall, in Gombe. Photograph by Hugo van Lawick, © National Geographic Society.

around, except that the slopes above the valley were very steep in places, and I slipped several times on the loose, gravelly soil.

I shall never forget the thrill of that first exploration. Soon after leaving camp I met a troop of baboons. They were afraid of the strange, white-skinned creature (that was I) and gave their barking alarm call, "Waa-hoo! Waa-hoo!" again and again. I left them, hoping that they would become used to me soon—otherwise, I thought, all the creatures of Gombe would be frightened. As I crossed a narrow ravine crowded with low trees and bushes I got very close to a beautiful red-gold bushbuck—a forest antelope about the size of a long-legged goat. I knew it was female because she had no horns. When she scented me she kept quite still for a moment and stared toward me with her big dark eyes. Then, with a loud barking call, she turned and bounded away.

When I got to one of the high ridges I looked down into the valley. There the forest was dark and thick. That was where I planned to go the next day to look for chimpanzees.

When I got back to camp it was dusk. Dominic had made a fire and was cooking our supper. That evening, and for the next four days, we had fresh food from Kigoma, but after that we ate out of cans. Louis had not managed to find very much money for our expedition, so our possessions were few and simple—a knife, fork, and spoon each, a couple of tin plates and tin mugs. But that was all we needed. After supper, Mum and I talked around our campfire, then snuggled into our two cots in the tent.

Early the next morning I set out to search for chimpanzees. I had been told by the British game ranger in charge of Gombe not to travel about the mountains by myself—except near camp. Otherwise, I had to take one of the game scouts with me. So I set off with Adolf. That first day we saw two chimps feeding in a tall tree. As soon as they saw us they leapt down and vanished. The next day we saw no chimps at all. Nor the day after. Nor the day after that.

A whole week went by before we found a very big tree full of tiny round red fruits that Adolf told me were called *msulula*. From the other side of the valley we could watch chimps arriving at the tree, feeding, then climbing down and vanishing into the forest. I decided to camp in the best viewing site so that I could see them first thing in the morning. I spent three days in that valley and I saw a lot of chimps. But they were too far away and the foliage of the tree was too thick. It was disappointing and frustrating, and I didn't have much to tell Mum when I got back.

There was another problem that I had to cope with—Adolf was very lazy. He was almost always late in the morning. I decided to try another man, Rashidi. He was far better and helped me a lot, showing me the trails through the forests and the best ways to move from one valley to the next. He had sharp eyes and spotted chimps from far away.

But even after several months, the chimps had not become used to us. They ran off if we got anywhere near to them. I begged the game ranger to let me move about the forests by myself. I promised that I would always tell Rashidi in which direction I was going, so that he would know where to look for me if I failed to turn up in the evening. The game ranger finally gave in. At last I could make friends with the chimpanzees in my own way.

Every morning I got up when I heard the alarm clock at 5:30 A.M. I ate a couple of slices of bread and had a cup of coffee from the Thermos flask. Then I set off, climbing to where I thought the chimps might be.

Most often, I went to the Peak. I discovered that from this high place I had a splendid view in all directions. I could see chimps moving in the trees and I could hear if they called. At first I watched from afar, through my binoculars, and never tried to get close. I knew that if I did, the chimps would run silently away.

Gradually I began to learn about the chimps' home and how they lived. I discovered that, most of the time, the chimps wandered about in small groups of six or less, not in a big troop like the baboons. Often a little group was made up of a mother with her children, or two or three adult males by themselves. Sometimes many groups joined together, especially when there was delicious ripe fruit on one big tree. When the chimps got together like that, they were very excited, made a lot of noise, and were easy to find.

Eventually I realized that the chimps I watched from the Peak were all part of one group—a community. There were about fifty chimps belonging to this community. They made use of three of the valleys to the north of the Kakombe Valley (where our tent was) and two valleys to the south. These valleys have lovely sounding names: Kasakela, Linda, and Rutanga in the north, Mkenke and Nyasanga in the south.

From the Peak I noted which trees the chimps were feeding in and then, when they had gone, I scrambled down and collected some of the leaves, flowers, or fruits so they could be identified later. I found that the chimps eat mostly fruits but also a good many kinds of leaves, blossoms, seeds, and stems. Later I would discover that they eat a variety of insects and sometimes hunt and kill prey animals to feed on meat.

During those months of gradual discovery, the chimps very slowly began to realize that I was not so frightening after all. Even so, it was almost a year before I could approach to within one hundred yards, and that is not really very close. The baboons got used to me much more quickly. Indeed, they became a nuisance around our camp by grabbing any food that we accidentally left lying on the table.

I began to learn more about the other creatures that shared the forests with the chimpanzees. There were four kinds of monkeys in addition to the baboons, and many smaller animals such as squirrels and mongooses. There was also a whole

variety of noctural (nighttime) creatures: por-
cupines and civets (creatures looking rather like
raccoons) and all manner of rats and mice. Only
a very few animals in the forests at Gombe were
potentially dangerous—mainly buffalo and leopards. Bush pigs can be dangerous too, but only if
you threaten them or their young. And, of
course, there are poisonous snakes—seven different kinds.

Once, as I arrived on the Peak in the early
morning before it was properly light, I saw the
dark shape of a large animal looming in front of
me. I stood quite still. My heart began to beat fast,
for I realized it was a buffalo. Many hunters fear
buffalo more than lions or elephants.

By a lucky chance the wind was blowing from
him to me, so he couldn't smell me. He was peacefully gazing in the opposite direction and chewing
his cud. He hadn't heard my approach—always I
try to move as quietly as I can in the bush. So,
though I was only ten yards from him, he had no
idea I was there. Very slowly I retreated.

Another time, as I was sitting on the Peak, I
heard a strange mewing sound. I looked around
and there, about fifteen yards away, a leopard
was approaching. I could just see the black and
white tip of its tail above the tall grass. It was
walking along the little trail that led directly to
where I sat.

63

Leopards are not usually dangerous unless they have been wounded. But I was frightened of them in those days—probably as a result of my experience with the leopard and the wolfhound two years before. And so, very silently, I moved away and looked for chimps in another valley.

Later I went back to the Peak. I found that, just like any cat, that leopard had been very curious. There, in the exact place where I had been sitting, he had left his mark—his droppings.

Most of the time, though, nothing more alarming than insects disturbed my vigils on the Peak. It began to feel like home. I carried a little tin trunk up there. In it I kept a kettle, some sugar and coffee, and a tin mug. Then, when I got tired from a long trek to another valley, I could make a drink in the middle of the day. I kept a blanket up there, too, and when the chimps slept near the Peak, I slept there, so that I could be close by in the morning. I loved to be up there at night, especially when there was a moon. If I heard the coughing grunt of a leopard, I just prayed and pulled the blanket over my head!

Chimps sleep all night, just as we do. From the Peak I often watched how they made their nests, or beds. First the chimp bent a branch down over some solid foundation, such as a fork or two parallel branches. Holding it in place with his feet, he then bent another over it. Then he folded the end of the first branch back over the second. And so on. He often ended up by picking lots of small, soft, leafy twigs to make a pillow. Chimps like their comfort! I've learned over the years that infants sleep in their nest with their mothers until they are about five years old or until the next baby is born and the older child has to make its own bed.

I never returned to camp before sunset. But even when I slept on the Peak, I first went down to have supper with Mum and tell her what I had seen that day. And she would tell me what she had been doing.

Mum set up a clinic. She handed out medicine to any of the local Africans, mostly fishermen, who were sick. Once she cured an old man who was very ill indeed. Word about this cure spread far and wide, and sometimes patients would walk for miles to get treatment from the wonderful white woman-doctor.

Her clinic was very good for me. It meant that the local people realized we wanted to help. When Mum had to go back to England after four months to manage things at home, the Africans wanted, in turn, to help me.

Of course, Mum worried about leaving me on my own. Dominic was a wonderful cook and great company, but he did sometimes get very drunk. He was not really reliable. So Louis Leakey asked

Hassan to come all the way from Lake Victoria to help with the boat and engine. It was lovely to see his handsome, smiling face again, and his arrival relieved Mum's mind no end.

Of course, I missed her after she'd gone, but I didn't have time to be lonely. There was so much to do.

Soon after she'd left, I got back one evening and was greeted by an excited Dominic. He told me that a big male chimp had spent an hour feeding on the fruit of one of the oil-nut palms growing in the camp clearing. Afterward he had climbed down, gone over to my tent, and taken the bananas that had just been put there for my supper.

This was fantastic news. For months the chimps had been running off when they saw me— now one had actually visited my camp! Perhaps he would come again.

The next day I waited, in case he did. What a luxury to lie in until 7:00 A.M. As the hours went by I began to fear that the chimp wouldn't come. But finally, at about four in the afternoon, I heard a rustling in the undergrowth opposite my tent, and a black shape appeared on the other side of the clearing.

I recognized him at once. It was the handsome male with the dense white beard. I had already named him David Greybeard. Quite calmly he climbed into the palm and feasted on its nuts. And

David Greybeard.
Photograph by
Hugo van Lawick,
© National Geo-
graphic Society.

then he helped himself to the bananas I had set out for him.

There were ripe palm nuts on that tree for another five days, and David Greybeard visited three more times and got lots of bananas.

A month later, when another palm tree in camp bore ripe fruit, David again visited us. And on one of those occasions he actually took a banana from my hand. I could hardly believe it.

From that time on things got easier for me. Sometimes when I met David Greybeard out in the forest, he would come up to see if I had a banana hidden in my pocket. The other chimps stared with amazement. Obviously I wasn't as dangerous as they had thought. Gradually they allowed me closer and closer.

It was David Greybeard who provided me with my most exciting observation. One morning, near the Peak, I came upon him squatting on a termite mound. As I watched, he picked a blade of grass, poked it into a tunnel in the mound, and then withdrew it. The grass was covered with termites all clinging on with their jaws. He picked them off with his lips and scrunched them up. Then he fished for more. When his piece of grass got bent, he dropped it, picked up a little twig, stripped the leaves off it, and used that.

I was really thrilled. David had used objects as tools! He had also changed a twig into something more suitable for fishing termites. He had actually *made* a tool. Before this observation, scientists had thought that only humans could make tools. Later I would learn that chimpanzees use more objects as tools than any creature except for us. This finding excited Louis Leakey more than any other.

In October the dry season ended and it began to rain. Soon the golden mountain slopes were covered with lush green grass. Flowers appeared, and the air smelled lovely. Most days it rained just a little. Sometimes there was a downpour. I loved being out in the forest in the rain. And I loved the cool evenings when I could lace the tent shut and make it cozy inside with a storm lantern. The only trouble was that everything got damp and grew mold. Scorpions and giant poisonous centipedes sometimes appeared in the tent—even, a few times, a snake. But I was lucky—I never got stung or bitten.

The chimpanzees often seemed miserable in the rain. They looked cold, and they shivered. Since they were clever enough to use tools, I was surprised that they had not learned to make shelters. Many of them got coughs and colds. Often, during heavy rain, they seemed irritable and bad tempered.

Once, as I walked through thick forest in a downpour, I suddenly saw a chimp hunched in front of me. Quickly I stopped. Then I heard a sound from above. I looked up and there was a big chimp there, too. When he saw me he gave a loud, clear wailing *wraaaah*—a spine-chilling call that is used to threaten a dangerous animal. To my right I saw a large black hand shaking a branch and bright eyes glaring threateningly through the foliage. Then came another savage *wraaaah* from behind. Up above, the big male began to sway the vegetation. I was surrounded. I crouched down, trying to appear as nonthreatening as possible.

Suddenly a chimp charged straight toward me.

His hair bristled with rage. At the last minute he swerved and ran off. I stayed still. Two more chimps charged nearby. Then, suddenly, I realized I was alone again. All the chimps had gone.

Only then did I realize how frightened I had been. When I stood up my legs were trembling! Male chimps, although they are only four feet tall when upright, are at least three times stronger than a grown man. And I weighed only about ninety pounds. I had become very thin with so much climbing in the mountains and only one meal a day. That incident took place soon after the chimps had lost their initial terror of me but before they had learned to accept me calmly as part of their forest world. If David Greybeard had been among them, they probably would not have behaved like that, I thought.

After my long days in the forests I looked forward to supper. Dominic always had it ready for me when I got back in the evenings. Once a month he went into Kigoma with Hassan. They came back with new supplies, including fresh vegetables and fruit and eggs. And they brought my mail—that was something I really looked forward to.

After supper I would get out the little notebook in which I had scribbled everything I had seen while watching the chimps during the day. I would settle down to write it all legibly into my journal. It was very important to do that every evening, while it was all fresh in my mind. Even on days when I climbed back to sleep near the chimps, I always wrote up my journal first.

Gradually, as the weeks went by, I began to recognize more and more chimpanzees as individuals. Some, like Goliath, William, and old Flo, I got to know well, because David Greybeard sometimes brought them with him when he visited camp. I always had a supply of bananas ready in case the chimps arrived.

Once you have been close to chimps for a while they are as easy to tell apart as your classmates. Their faces look different, and they have different characters. David Greybeard, for example, was a calm chimp who liked to keep out of trouble. But he was also very determined to get his own way. If he arrived in camp and couldn't find any bananas, he would walk into my tent and search. Afterward, all was chaos. It looked as though some burglar had raided the place! Goliath had a much more excitable, impetuous temperament. William, with his long-shaped face, was shy and timid.

Old Flo was easy to identify. She had a bulbous nose and ragged ears. She came to camp with her infant daughter, whom I named Fifi, and her juvenile son, Figan. Sometimes adolescent Faben came, too. It was from Flo that I first learned that in the wild, female chimps have only one baby

71

The author and David Greybeard. Photograph by Hugo van Lawick, © National Geographic Society.

every five or six years. The older offspring, even after they have become independent, still spend a lot of time with their mothers, and all the different family members help one another.

Flo also taught me that female chimps do not have just one mate. One day she came to my camp with a pink swelling on her rump. This was a sign that she was ready for mating. She was followed by a long line of suitors. Many of them had never visited my camp before, and they were scared. But they were so attracted to Flo that they overcame their fear in order to keep close to her. She allowed them all to mate with her at different times.

Soon after the chimps had begun to visit my camp, the National Geographic Society, which was giving Louis money for my research, sent a photographer to Gombe to make a film. Hugo van Lawick was a Dutch baron. He loved and respected animals just as I did, and he made a wonderful movie. One year later, in England, we got married.

By then I had left Gombe for a while, to start my own studies at Cambridge University. I hated to leave, but I knew I would soon be back. I had promised Louis that I would work hard and get my Ph.D. degree.

After I got the degree, Hugo and I went back to Gombe together. It was a very exciting time, as Flo had just had a baby, little Flint. That was the first wild chimpanzee infant that I ever saw close up, nearly four years after I had begun my research.

Flo came very often to camp looking for bananas. Fifi, now six years old, and Figan, five years older, were still always with her. Fifi loved her new baby brother. When he was four months old she was allowed to play with and groom him. Sometimes Flo let her carry him when they moved through the forest. During that time, Fifi

73

Fifi looking for the bananas we sometimes hid under our shirts. Photograph by Hugo van Lawick, © National Geographic Society.

learned a lot about how to be a good mother.

Flint learned to walk and climb when he was six months old. And he learned to ride on his mother's back during travel, instead of always clinging on underneath. He gradually spent more time playing with his two older brothers. They were always very gentle with him. So were other youngsters of the community. They had to be, for if Flo thought any other chimps were too rough, she would charge over and threaten or even attack them.

74

MY LIFE WITH THE CHIMPANZEES

I watched how Flint gradually learned to use more and more of the different calls and gestures that chimpanzees use to communicate with each other. Some of these gestures are just like ours — holding hands, embracing, kissing, patting one another on the back. They mean about the same, too. And although they do not make up a language the way human words do, all the different calls do help the chimpanzees know what is happening, even if they are far away when they hear the sounds. Each call (there are at least thirty, perhaps more) means something different.

Flo was the top-ranked female of her community and could dominate all the others. But she could not boss any of the males. In chimpanzee society, males are the dominant sex. Among the males themselves, there is a social order, and one male at the top is the boss.

The first top-ranking male I knew was Goliath. Then, in 1964, Mike took over. He did this by using his brain. He would gather up one or two empty kerosene cans from my camp and hit and kick them ahead of him as he charged toward a group of adult males. It was a spectacular performance and made a lot of noise. The other chimps fled. So Mike didn't need to fight to get to the top — which was just as well, as he was a very small chimp. He was top male for six years.

The adult males spend a lot of time in each

other's company. They often patrol the boundaries of their territory and may attack chimpanzees of different communities if they meet. These conflicts are very brutal, and the victim may die. Only young females can move from one community to another without being hurt. In fact, the big males sometimes go out looking for such females and try to take them back into their own territory.

As the months went by, I learned more and more. I recorded more and more details when I watched the chimpanzees. Instead of writing the information in notebooks, I started to use a little tape recorder. Then I could keep my eyes on the chimps all the time. By the end of each day there was so much typing to be done that I found I couldn't do it all myself. I needed an assistant to help. Soon, with even more chimps coming to camp, I needed other people to help with the observations.

There were always more fascinating things to watch and record, more people to help write everything down. What had started as a little camp for Mum and me ended up, six years later, as a research center, where students could come and collect information for their degrees. I was the director.

In 1967, something special happened. For me it was the most important event of my life. I had a baby of my own.

CHAPTER 7

The Africans said my son should have been called Simba, Swahili for lion. This is why. Just before he was born, I was camping with Hugo in Ngorongoro Crater. The crater is the inside of a giant volcano that blew its top off millions of years ago. Now it is one hundred square miles of grassland and trees, a lake, and some little rivers. It is one of the most beautiful places in the world. And it is famous for its wildlife, especially its beautiful black-maned lions.

One evening, Hugo and I were waiting for our cook, Anyango, to walk over with supper. Suddenly the quiet African night was filled with shouting, then with banging and clattering sounds as though someone was throwing pots and pans. After a few moments of silence we heard the sound of ripping canvas, more shouting, and more banging.

Hugo put his head out to see what on earth was

going on. But he quickly ducked back inside and zipped up the front of the tent. He looked a bit pale. "There's a lion out there," he said. "It's between us and the Land Rover."

In the bush you always park your car close to your tent so that you can leap into it if there is an emergency. If the lion was between the tent and the car, we knew it was very close indeed.

"It must have ripped open the kitchen tent," said Hugo.

"Or Anyango's, or Thomas's," I said. Thomas, who helped with odd jobs around the camp, had a little tent next to Anyango's. Both were near the kitchen tent.

Suppose the lion ripped open *our* tent. We decided to light the small gas stove. If a lion tried to enter we would light newspapers and wave them in its face.

A few moments later we heard racing footsteps. The car door opened and slammed shut. Almost at once there were more running footsteps and again the car door opened and slammed shut. Obviously Anyango and Thomas had reached safety.

Hugo cautiously zipped open the tent. There was no sign of a lion. Hugo scrambled into the car. He inched it forward, and I got in, too. Anyango and Thomas told us there were three lions. We switched on the headlights and looked for them.

Soon we saw them—young males with their manes just beginning to sprout. We began to try herding them away from our camp. At first they didn't want to go. They were curious and a bit playful. But eventually they wandered off into the night. We drove back and—oh, dear!—the first thing we saw was the flickering of flames. We had left the front flap of our tent loose, and the wind had blown it against the stove.

Luckily we had a fire extinguisher in the car and soon put the fire out. Then we heard the story from Anyango and Thomas.

Anyango was just going to serve our supper. Suddenly he looked up and saw a lion's head framed in the entrance of the tent. Yelling loudly, he hurled saucepans and frying pans at it. The head vanished. Anyango called a warning to Thomas, who was resting in his little tent. Quickly Thomas closed the flap. But to his horror, a moment later the whole tent shook, and a great gash appeared in the side of it. A lion's head peered in through the opening. Thomas, like Anyango, pelted the intruder with everything he could see.

Fortunately, instead of getting angry, the lions wandered away. Peering cautiously into the night, Anyango, with his sharp African eyes, saw the third lion—the one who had visited Hugo and me—following his two companions behind the tents. That was when he and Thomas decided to run for safety. It was silly of them, because lions, like cats, love to chase running, fast-moving things. But they were lucky. They made it.

Obviously we could not sleep in our torn and burned tents that night. We ate our supper—which was still hot. Then we packed up a few essentials and drove to a little log cabin nearby. We had stayed there before. The young couple who had been living in it had just left, so we knew it was empty. Imagine how we felt when, as we drove toward it, we saw a very large black-maned lion on the veranda! And behind the cabin was his lioness, feasting on a freshly caught antelope!

Eventually the male left. We managed to get into the cabin without disturbing the lioness, and Anyango and Thomas bolted themselves into the little wooden kitchen hut for the night.

No wonder they thought that my son, born so soon afterward, should have been called Simba! As it was, he became known as Grub to his family and closest friends. There was no very good reason for this. His real name is Hugo Eric Louis.

When Grub was a tiny baby, Hugo and I were studying hyenas in Ngorongoro Crater. You probably think of hyenas as skulking, cowardly scavengers, waiting for scraps left by the lions. Don't believe it! They are great hunters, going after wildebeests and zebras, as well as smaller

Grub taking a bath in the forest. Photograph © Hugo van Lawick.

creatures. Quite often, especially in the crater, they actually lose *their* kills to scavenging lions. They try to defend their prey fiercely at such times. They do also feed on the remains of lions' kills, but they do not always wait patiently until the lion has finished. If there are enough of them, they try to drive the lions away.

Hyenas are actually very interesting creatures. Like chimps, they wander around in little groups of friendly individuals. Like chimps, they have very distinct personalities and fascinating behavior. Like chimps, they are territorial and may kill hyenas from neighboring clans. The biggest difference in their social behavior is that females are dominant in hyena society, whereas males are dominant in the world of the chimp.

I loved studying those Ngorongoro hyenas. At night, when there was a moon, I would drive our VW camper to a hyena den where there were one or two tiny black cubs. Grub was usually asleep in the back of the car. As dusk settled, other, older cubs would begin to appear. They were coming to play with the little ones, the ones who were not old enough to go visiting.

What wonderful games went on around those dens in the moonlight! Sometimes the cubs played tag with an ostrich feather or an old bone. They had mock battles and tumbled over and over, wrestling and biting.

After hunting, late at night, the hyena mothers would visit the dens. They would suckle their cubs and sometimes bring back a large bone or a whole head from a kill. And there were times when even the biggest and fattest of the mothers, Mrs. Stink and Baggage, for example, would start to play, chasing each other and the cubs around in circles, their fat bellies almost touching the ground.

During the months I spent in the crater and afterward, on the Serengeti when Hugo was film-ing the wild dogs, there were other people at

Grub in Ngorongoro Crater. Photograph © Hugo van Lawick.

Gombe watching the chimpanzees. I used to talk to them on a two-way radio almost every day. And quite often, we went to Gombe to spend some time there ourselves.

But when Grub was small, we had to be very careful. Chimpanzees, as I have said, are hunters. I knew that many years before I had arrived at Gombe, chimpanzees had taken two African babies for food. Of course, that seems shocking to us. But from the chimps' point of view it is no different to take a human baby than a baboon baby. Some African tribes in West and Central Africa love to eat chimpanzees.

Anyway, I took good care to always guard *my* baby very safely when he came to Gombe. Before he could walk, we built a "cage" for him. It was a safe place for his cot, inside the little one-roomed house where Hugo and I lived.

Then Grub began to walk. We could no longer keep him in his safe cage. So we built another house, down on the beach where the chimpanzees only sometimes roamed. We constructed a big, caged-in veranda where Grub could play safely.

Grub helping to put up the tent in Ngorongoro Crater. Photograph © Hugo van Lawick.

When Grub was outside, he was always with someone—often with me. When he was small, I more or less stopped working with the chimps. I went up to the chimp camp most days, but just to talk to the students, and to see the chimps—Flo and her family and all my other friends. Then I went down to my office in the house on the beach and got on with all the work of running a research center: writing reports, writing articles for scientific books, requesting money so that the work could go on. I had about twelve students and assistants then. It was a lot of work.

Then, after lunch, I spent the rest of the day with Grub. We went for walks and looked at books and talked about things. Because Hugo and I didn't want to send him away to school, we found a tutor for him when he was older. He had regular lessons every morning.

When Grub was seven years old, Hugo and I separated and divorced. Hugo's work, photographing and filming, took him all over the place. And I felt that it was important for me to spend most of my time at Gombe. We stayed good friends, but it was sad, especially for Grub. If I could live that part of my life over again, I would try very hard to work things out differently.

Hugo and I both married again. I married an Englishman, Derek Bryceson. He was the director of Tanzania National Park. Derek had

Grub and the author at Olduvai Gorge. Photograph © Hugo van Lawick.

been a fighter pilot in World War II, where he flew Hurricanes. He was shot down in the Middle East when he was just nineteen. After that he was almost completely paralyzed from the waist down. He got about, but with great difficulty, by using a stick—and willpower.

To visit Gombe, Derek used to fly from his

home in Dar es Salaam in a little single-engine four-seater Cessna plane called Mike Whisky. He sometimes flew her himself, but only when she was airborne. He couldn't land or take off, because you have to use your legs and feet to keep the plane straight and to brake. Sometimes Grub and I flew with him to visit one of Tanzania's other national parks.

One day we flew from Dar es Salaam to a lovely wild park called Ruaha. Derek and the pilot were sitting together in the front. Suddenly they noticed something scary. A little plume of smoke was creeping out from the instrument panel! We were flying over rugged country, and there was nowhere to land until we got to the bush airstrip at Ruaha. That was forty-five minutes away.

Derek told us we should try not to worry. We talked of other things. The little wisp of smoke didn't go away. But it didn't get any worse, either.

At last we got to Ruaha. The pilot came down to land, but there was a herd of zebras on the strip. So he pulled up and circled around.

To this day I can't imagine why, after all that time, the pilot suddenly lost his nerve. Instead of circling right around and coming down on the airstrip, he tried to land among the trees on the far side of the Ruaha River. *Wham!* We hit the ground. One wing smashed into a tree. We slewed around. The plane crashed on through the bushes and banged into another tree. Finally we came to a stop. The pilot opened his door, yelled, "Get out quickly—she's going up in flames," and was gone! I told Grub to follow him. But the door on Derek's side would open only about two inches. Then it hit the ground. The wheel on that side had buckled, so the plane sat at a crazy angle, the opposite wing high in the air.

For a few moments I panicked. How on earth could Derek, with his almost paralyzed legs, get out of the plane before it caught fire? Then he told me to relax, that there would be no fire. And slowly he managed to pull himself up and out through the other door.

After getting out of the plane, we had to cross the Ruaha River to get to park headquarters on the other side. We could have waited for a car to come around via the hand-operated ferry, but that was some way upriver and would have taken about thirty minutes. So we decided that despite the big crocodiles in the river, we would risk it and wade across. After all, if God had allowed us to survive the crash, surely He would not allow crocodiles to eat us! And He didn't!

We arrived at the rest house tired and wet, but thankful to be alive and unharmed. By then my legs had begun to shake from delayed shock! We were all glad to sit down and have a nice hot, strong cup of tea.

Those trips to Tanzania's beautiful parks were wonderful, and I learned more and more about many different animals. But I still spent almost all my time at Gombe with the chimps and with the students who came from the United States and Europe to help with the observations or to collect information for their master's or doctoral degrees.

In the middle of one night in 1975, some African rebels from Zaire crossed the lake in a motorboat and captured four of the students who were working at Gombe. They tied them up and took them back over the lake.

It was very frightening. We didn't know where they had gone for quite a long time. We didn't even know if they were alive. All the rest of us had to leave Gombe and go to Dar es Salaam, the capital of Tanzania. Grub and I joined Derek in his house on the shore of the Indian Ocean, and many of the students squeezed into our little guest house. It was terrible, waiting to know what would happen. But eventually, after secret negotiations, a big ransom was paid to the rebels, and the students were all released.

During those weeks of waiting, Derek and I twice visited Gombe to try to encourage the Tanzanian field staff who were carrying on with observing the chimpanzees. They did a wonderful job, but they needed a lot of guidance and help at

Grub and Derek sitting on the veranda of the house in Dar es Salaam.

first. But for Derek, the chimpanzee research might have ended then.

Derek was a nationalized Tanzanian. He knew Swahili as well as he knew English. And he was liked and respected by almost all Tanzanians, including the Kigoma officials and my own field staff. He helped me to build up a new research center, where almost all the observations were made by the Tanzanian field staff.

The following year Grub was nine. He went to live with my mother in England and went to school close by. He slept in the room where I had slept from the time I was about twelve. Grub and I were together every holiday, except for the time he spent with his father.

CHAPTER 8

Over the twenty-eight years that I have worked at Gombe I have gotten to know many chimpanzees. Some of those I have known only slightly—because they were shy and I didn't see them often, or because they died soon after I first met them. Others I have gotten to know well. Because chimpanzees are so like humans, and because each has his or her own unique character, there have been some individuals that I have not liked very much, some that were just okay, and some that I have liked very much indeed.

I really loved old Flo. And because she came so often to my camp in the early days, I learned a great deal about chimpanzee behavior during the hours that I spent with her and her family.

In 1964, when Flint was born, Flo was the top-ranking female. In chimp society, adult males are always able to dominate females. Flo couldn't boss them around, but she could boss all the other

Flo feeding on termites. Photograph by Hugo van Lawick, © National Geographic Society.

females. Even though she was already old (chimps live to be fifty years old, and Flo was probably about thirty-five then), she would always charge fearlessly to Flint's defense if he needed her help. Moreover, the rest of his family —especially Fifi, but also Figan and even adult Faben—helped to protect little Flint. He became very self-assured. He would threaten chimps older and stronger than he was, because he knew that if they dared to retaliate, his mother, his sister, or one of his brothers would rush to help him. By the time he was four years old, Flint could best be described as a "spoiled brat."

Then came the beginning of a bad time for Flint—Flo began to wean him. When he wanted to suckle, she pushed him away. When he jumped on her back during travel, she shrugged him off. Many youngsters become upset during weaning. Often they throw tantrums—hurling themselves about, screaming until they almost choke. Flint, because he was so spoiled, threw truly awful tantrums. He even hit and bit his mother. Indeed, he was so violent that Flo had not managed to wean him by the time her next baby was born.

Most youngsters begin to make their own night nests when their baby brothers or sisters are born. But Flint insisted on pushing in with Flo and his new baby sister, Flame. When Flo tried to stop him, he cried until she gave in.

Flint insisted on riding on Flo's back even though little Flame was clinging on below. Because part of Flo's attention now went to the new baby, Flint became upset and frustrated. He behaved like a jealous human child and even tried to push in and suckle along with the baby. When Flo stopped him (for she had not enough milk for him as well), he threw another tantrum. Then he sulked. When Flo groomed the baby, Flint often pulled her hand away and asked her to groom him, instead.

One day I found Flo lying on the ground. She was very sick. Baby Flame had disappeared and

Flo, Fifi, Flint, and the author. Photograph by Hugo van Lawick, © National Geographic Society.

we never knew what happened to her. To our relief, Flo eventually recovered. And Flint, now that he had his mother's undivided attention, quickly regained his former high spirits. But he went on sharing Flo's nest, he continued to ride on her back, and he constantly demanded that she groom him. And she always gave in.

Any normal youngster of eight years would have begun spending time away from his mother and traveling with the big males—especially if he had an older brother who would keep an eye on him. And Flint had two big brothers. But Flint was not normal. He was still pathetically dependent on Flo. And she, by this time, looked very, very ancient. Her teeth were worn down to the gum, her hair was thin and brownish in color (instead of glossy black), and she was as shrunken and frail-looking as a little old lady. When Flint tried to ride on her back, she collapsed, so he had to walk. But he still slept with her at night. Because she was weak and unable to keep up with the other chimps, she and Flint were on their own together for a great deal of the time.

When old Flo died in 1972, it was a very sad day for me. I had known her so long. She died crossing the clear, fast-flowing Kakombe Stream. She looked quite peaceful. It was as if, quite suddenly, her old heart had just stopped beating. I remember looking down at her and thinking that I had lost an old friend and that Gombe would never be quite the same again.

For Flint, his mother's death was a terrible blow from which he never recovered—it was as though by losing her he had lost his whole world. Hunched and miserable, he sat on the bank of the stream near Flo's dead body. From time to time he moved down to inspect her, desperately searching, it seemed, for some sign of life. He stared at her, and sometimes he even pulled at her hand as though begging her to groom him, to comfort him, as she had when she was alive.

But Flo never moved. Her body lay still, cold and dead, and finally Flint moved away. He fell into a deep depression. He ate almost nothing, he stayed mostly by himself, and in this state of grief he fell sick. This often happens when we are very miserable, because then the body's defenses against disease are weakened.

Flint never recovered from that illness. Of course we tried to help him. We took him food. We stayed beside him so that he would not feel so alone. But nothing did any good, and about a month after Flo died, Flint died, too. Because his mother had been too old to force him to become independent, Flint, it seemed, was unable to face life without her.

Still we were left with Faben, Figan, and Fifi. It was a really exciting day when Fifi, at thirteen years of age, had her first baby. It was a son, whom I named Freud. What sort of a mother would Fifi be? As time went on we soon found that she was the same kind of mother as Flo had always been—affectionate and protective, tolerant and playful. Some of Fifi's behavior was inherited— instinctive. Some she had learned from watching Flo handling Flint and Flame. And some she had acquired by practice, from the days when she had been allowed to care for Flint.

When Freud was five years old, his brother, Frodo, was born. Freud loved him. He played with him and carried him, just as Fifi had done with her new brother twelve years before. Frodo watched everything that big brother Freud did. Once he gazed, his eyes big with wonder, as Freud played with young baboons, chased after them, then threatened them by waving a big stick. Afterward Frodo wanted to do the same—but he couldn't even lift the stick from the ground! Because he was always trying to copy Freud, Frodo was very precocious.

When Frodo was five years old, Fifi gave birth to a daughter, Fanni. Frodo was fascinated by

Fifi plays with Frodo.

Fifi and Fanni.

Fanni, just as Freud had been by him. Frodo was often very rough, though, when he played with his sister. But she didn't seem to mind. And then, four and a half years later, along came Flossie. Freud, the eldest, was by then a fully adult male. But he was still spending time with his family and often played gently with both of his small sisters.

When I am at Gombe I love to be with Fifi and her family in the forest. If I know where they slept the night before, I get up very early and arrive at their nests when it is just beginning to get light. Then I follow them, sometimes for a few hours, sometimes for the whole day.

98

MY LIFE WITH THE CHIMPANZEES

It is not easy to follow chimps for a long time. There are some trails at Gombe where you can walk upright, but the chimps don't use these very often. They go along their own pathways, moving easily through thick tangles of thorny under-growth. To follow, you must crawl after them on all fours, or even wriggle along on your tummy, like a snake. Thorns catch at your clothes, your hair, and your skin. Vines catch around the buckles of your shoes. As you struggle to pull free, you see the black shapes ahead vanishing, and you almost cry with frustration.

If you are lucky, you find the chimps again when you emerge from your battles with the vegetation. There they are, feeding peacefully in a tree, or resting quietly on the ground and groom-ing each other. Then you can relax and gather energy for the next journey.

The Tanzanian field staff are wonderful at following the chimps, even through the most difficult places, up the steepest and most treach-erous slopes. But even they get defeated when the chimps cross a narrow, steep-sided valley by swinging from tree to tree, or when they climb a sheer cliff by shinnying up slender vines, or if they suddenly decide to travel really fast and silently.

However difficult it is to follow them, however much you get scratched and bruised, it's always worth it if you can keep up. Often, after a really difficult scramble, you are rewarded by a particularly interesting observation—such as the time when a group of males called out, some distance from Fifi and her family. She didn't want to join them. But Freud did. And even though he was quite grown up, he didn't want to go without Mom. Not that day. So what did he do? He went over to baby Flossie, who was quietly playing by herself. He gathered her up and, when she clung to his belly, set off toward the males. Then Fifi had to follow!

I wonder if Freud will become an alpha—that is, a top-ranking male—like his uncle, Figan. The story of how Figan got to the top is interesting. It is one more story that I have learned during the years of watching the different members of the Flo family.

I have already told you how Mike got to the top by hitting empty tin cans ahead during his charging displays. One day, when Mike was probably about thirty-five years old, he was overthrown by a very big and aggressive male called Humphrey. But Humphrey, despite his size, didn't last for long—only for eighteen months. And then Figan became top male.

Like Mike, Figan was small. Like Mike, he defeated larger rivals by using his brain. How did he do this? By deliberately making use of the friendly relationship that he had with brother Faben. Faben was stricken with polio during the epidemic of 1966 and lost the use of one arm. But even with a paralyzed arm, he was a good ally. He had learned how to do magnificent upright charging displays. Figan knew that if he challenged one of the older males, Faben almost always would come rushing up to help him. And

Faben walking upright after being stricken by polio. Photograph © Hugo van Lawick.

101

so Figan only confronted the much bigger and heavier Humphrey when Faben was in the same group. Then he charged toward Humphrey, threatened him again and again, and Faben usually joined in so that it was two against one. Humphrey became more and more tense when the brothers were around, and Figan became more and more self-confident.

One evening, something exciting happened. Figan was with a very big group of chimps. Faben was there, too, and so was Humphrey. As the sun sank, the chimps started to make their nests.

Suddenly Figan began to leap wildly through the branches. There were loud screams from the chimps as they rushed out of his way.

All at once, as though made brave by his display of power, Figan leapt down onto Humphrey, who was already lying in his nest, and attacked him. Humphrey, screaming loudly, pulled away from Figan and dropped to the ground. Figan followed, attacked him again, and then climbed back into the tree. Presently Humphrey climbed back too and made a second nest.

But Figan had not finished yet. Just when everything was peaceful, he again leapt through the branches and attacked Humphrey a second time. Poor Humphrey! He sat screaming until it was almost dark, then cautiously climbed back into the tree and made his third nest. Never again, for the rest of his life, did he try to dominate Figan. And so Flo's son, when he was about twenty-three years old, became top-ranking male. He was alpha until he died ten years later.

I have told you stories about the life histories of one family of chimpanzees. Soon I hope to write more books telling about some of my other chimpanzee friends, for I have learned so many fascinating things over the years. Of course, the more time I spend in writing, the less time I have to be with the chimps at Gombe. But it is very important for scientists to share their information with people. I want everyone to understand how wonderful chimpanzees really are.

I spend about four months of each year at Gombe watching the chimps, four months writing in Dar es Salaam, and the rest of the year raising money to pay for the research at Gombe. In Dar, I write in Derek's house by the Indian Ocean. I now live here alone except for my three dogs. Derek died of cancer after we had been married only a few years.

Every spring comes my annual lecture tour in the United States. Even if the research had all the money needed, I would probably still go around and give talks, because I want to share what I know with as many people as possible. I have been very lucky in my life. I have known the excitement of watching wild, free animals. Thou-

Melissa with her twins. © National Geographic Society.

sands of people can never know that joy. But at least I can tell them about it.

My trips around the USA are crazy! I race from place to place, with never enough time anywhere. After one of these hectic tours I go back to England, to the dear old red brick house, The Birches, where I grew up. Danny is not there anymore, but she lived to be ninety-seven, and was mentally alert right to the end. Uncle Eric died too, but not until he was eighty-eight. And Mum, Olly, and Audrey are still there. We have a wonderful dog, Cida, who I take for long walks when I'm home.

We go on the cliffs and follow the routes I used to take with Rusty.

When I get back to Tanzania I set off for Gombe as soon as I can. First I always spend a little time in Dar with my friends and helpers and with my dogs—Cinderella, Ripal and Seranda. Of course they are well looked after while I am away, but they love it when their mistress gets home.

Sometimes it is not easy to get to Gombe. Planes are often canceled at the last minute. The train journey takes almost three days. When I do get back, there are usually quite a lot of problems to sort out. Tanzania is a poor country, and it is difficult to get enough medicine, gasoline, building materials, and so on. There have been times when it has been hard to get enough food.

But all my problems fade away when I follow the chimps deep into the forest and sit with them. The birds sing. The wind whispers in the leaves. Little lizards move up and down the old trunks of trees. That, for me, is like a visit to heaven.

I especially love being in the forests in the wet season. The ground is soft, so I can walk silently. The vegetation is green and lush. There are flowers everywhere and the air is full of lovely smells. In the dry season there always seem to be visitors around. But in the rainy months I am usually at Gombe by myself. And that, for me, is best.

105

Searching for chimpanzees. Photograph by Hugo van Lawick, © National Geographic Society.

I am writing these words as I sit in my house on the beach at Gombe. It is softly raining outside. It is getting late, and soon I shall have to light my little oil lamp. There is a big fig tree growing over the house. Earlier I followed the oldest male chimp, Evered, here. He is about thirty-five years old. He fed on the figs for forty-three minutes, then climbed back up the mountain slope. I left him and came in out of the rain. Presently I shall light a small wood fire and cook some rice and beans, tomatoes, and onions.

Yesterday evening was fine. I sat out on the

beach after supper in the light of the full moon and thought back over the past fifty years of my life. What would I do differently, I wondered, if I could start all over again? There are some things I've done that I wish I hadn't. And there are things I haven't done that I wish I had. Mostly, though, I would want my life to be just the same.

Of course, bad things happen. People I trusted let me down. And there were times when *I* let down people who trusted *me*. That is much worse. It's okay to be mad at someone else—it's terrible to be mad at yourself. But you learn from all those things, and you try not to do them or let them occur again.

Suppose someone asks me: "Which were the worst happenings in your life? And which were the best?"

Well, there are two kinds of bad things that can take place. There are the things that just happen to you, out of the blue, that you can't do anything about. Such as when Derek got cancer and died, or when the students were kidnapped from Gombe. The other kind of bad thing is the kind that is your fault, or partly your fault. Getting divorced was one. So was hurting people I didn't want to hurt—because I didn't or couldn't do things they wanted me to do, or I said things that made them unhappy.

And the best happenings? There are two kinds

107

of these, too. Some things are simply the result of good fortune. The best of them, for me, was to have such a wonderful mother and family. That was real luck. So was being born with such a strong and healthy body and mind. It is only too easy to destroy a good body—with smoking, drugs, eating junk foods, and so on. But if you are born with a faulty body, it's often hard or impossible to make it well. The third really important piece of good luck was having a friend whose parents moved to Kenya—so that I could meet Louis Leakey.

The other kinds of good things are those that you *make* happen through your own efforts. Actually going to Africa because I earned the money, and getting a job with Louis because I had learned so much about animals that he was impressed, were two of these. Another was succeeding with the chimps in the early days. I refused to give up, even when it seemed very difficult.

Suppose someone else asks me: "What have you contributed to the world?"

Well, I have raised a wonderful son.

I have made it possible for many gifted students to work at Gombe. They are all over the world now, and they continue to do good research. They say that being at Gombe, with the chimps, was very important for them.

I, along with others, have helped people to

understand what truly wonderful animals chimpanzees are. This has helped the chimpanzees. For one thing, chimps are treated far better in most zoos now than they were in bygone years. I have helped certain zoos to raise money so that their chimps could be moved out of small cages into nice outdoor enclosures. And I have tried to think of ways to improve life for captive chimps.

I have started an exciting new project with captive chimps. This is called ChimpanZoo. Students and keepers and volunteers study chimp behavior in zoo groups, just as I study their behavior at Gombe. About fourteen zoos in North America are already taking part, and others hope to do so soon. Even zoos in Europe now want to join. What a lot we shall learn in the years to come! Best of all, in all of the zoos taking part, the lives of the chimps have been much improved. Most of them are already in big enclosures, and those still in small cages will soon be moved out of them. All the chimps have more interesting food—lots of different kinds of fruit and vegetables. And they have things to do so they are not too bored.

What a lot we shall learn from this program in the years to come! You may be able to help with ChimpanZoo when you are older, if you are interested.

Because of our work with the chimps, we understand more about humans than we did

109

before. We know we are not as different from the rest of the animal kingdom as we once thought we were. We know that chimps can do lots of things that we used to think only humans could do. They can, for example, use and make tools. They can be taught at least three hundred signs of the sign language for the deaf, and using these signs they can make sentences and "talk" to humans.

Of course, in some ways we are different from other animals. With our human speech we can talk about the past and make plans for the future. We have free will and can choose to do something because we know it is right, even if we don't want to do it at all.

And what now? What are my plans for the future? First of all, I shall carry on at Gombe for as long as I can. I hope there will be people to study the chimps there, and money to pay them, long after I am too old to climb the hills. I want to know what sort of mothers Fanni and Flossie will be. I want to know if Frodo will become top-ranking male, as I suspect he will. And I have lots and lots of other questions.

Right now my most important goal is to try to make things better for the chimps and other animals that we use for medical research. I shall talk about this in the next chapter.

In some ways, perhaps, the most important part of my life is still ahead of me.

CHAPTER 9

When I was your age I didn't think much about what I would do when I grew up. I knew that, somehow, I would go to Africa. I knew that in some way I would work with animals. But I was too busy living and learning to care very much about the future. Too busy reading books, watching the birds and insects in the garden, being with Rusty. Too busy organizing the Alligator Club, climbing trees, and riding horses. And too busy having fun. We laughed a lot in my family. We still do.

What about you? Do you know what you want to do when you're grown-up? If you do, you are lucky. Most young people today don't know what they want to do, even when they have finished school. As I write this, my son is twenty-one. He's studying anthropology. But he doesn't know what he wants to do when he leaves college. Not yet.

Suppose you are one of the unusual ones. Let's

Grub and the author at Gombe. Photograph © Mary Ellen Mark.

say that you want to work with animals, as I did. Can you prepare for that in any way, now?

Of course you can. You can watch animals and see what they do. You can write notes about what you see. And you can ask those *why, how,* and *what for* questions that we talked about in Chapter 1. Some answers you will find by watching. And some you can find only by looking them up in a book or asking a knowledgeable teacher. Whatever you do, don't do anything that hurts or frightens the animal you are interested in.

You can go on nature walks, as I used to. Even if

you live in a city, there are parks or gardens where you can watch some kind of animal. Remember, I began with worms! You can collect a caterpillar and keep it in a jar until it turns into a chrysalis. But you must find out what it eats, and you must remember to keep it supplied with fresh food. (Put the stem of a leaf spray in water, in a narrow-necked container, such as a bottle, so the caterpillar can't fall in and drown. This way the food will stay fresh longer.) You will hate yourself if you forget to provide food and find your caterpillar all dried up. It will need water, too—just a few drops sprinkled on the leaves will do. You will see how it changes its skin as it eats more and gets fatter.

When it makes itself a hard case and becomes a chrysalis, you should put this where you can see it every day. It's so easy to forget, when you don't have to look after it anymore. But it is wonderful to see the butterfly or moth emerging and watch its crumpled wings become flat and strong. Then the beautiful creature that you have raised can fly out into the sunlight. (Or into the night, if it is a moth.)

It is even more exciting to watch a pair of birds as they go about making a nest. Don't get too close, though, or they will leave the site, especially during the building and the brooding. But watching and making notes on the whole of the rearing

113

will give you a real feeling of accomplishment. I used to make drawings. And once I was really lucky. A robin—the little British bird with a red breast, not the big American robin—came to my windowsill one winter while I was sick in bed. I put crumbs out every day. We fixed up a bird table, a board sticking out from the sill. That robin got so tame he would come and take crumbs from my bed, because I left the window open, even when it was very cold. In the spring he brought his mate, and they made a nest in my bedroom—in the bookcase right near my Doctor Doolittle books! That was truly fabulous.

Do you have a dog? Suppose he wants to go outside. How does he ask? Does he bark or whine at the door while looking at you? That's easy to understand. But dogs can ask in other ways. Perhaps he or she comes up to you (or to another member of your family) and lays his head on your knee. Or he looks at you, gives a tiny whine, and wags his tail. Or he starts to pant, getting louder and louder. Or he becomes restless and walks about a lot. If he gives up in despair because none of the dumb humans seem to understand or care, he may lie down. But then, when you do get up, he will probably become very excited and start bounding about.

I know a black poodle who will fetch his mistress's outdoor shoes and bring them to her, one by one, when *he* wants to go out. A lot of dogs will bring you their leashes. Konrad Lorenz describes another method. His dog needed to go out, very urgently, in the middle of the night. She couldn't wake Lorenz by whining or scratching the door— her usual way of asking. So she leapt up onto his bed (which she was strictly not allowed to do) and actually dug him out of the blankets and rolled him onto the floor!

You can watch the dogs of your friends. See how long a list you can make of the different ways they "talk" to their human companions—and to other dogs. You can do just the same with cats.

Dr. Doolittle's parrot, Polynesia, tells us that in order to learn animal language we must have "powers of observation." We must be able to notice "small things about birds and animals— the way they walk and move their heads and flip their wings—the way they sniff the air and twitch their whiskers and wiggle their tails."

Of course, you don't have to become an ethologist to study or work with animals. There are lots of other "ologists" to choose from! You could become a zoologist, a biologist, an anthropologist, or an ecologist. And there are even more. You can look up what they all mean in a dictionary. Or perhaps you want to become a veterinarian, work in a kennel, or work with horses.

Remember one thing. If you are really and truly

determined to work with animals, somehow, either now or later, you will one day find a way to do it. But you have to want it desperately, work hard, and be quick to take an opportunity.

Perhaps, though, you don't want to study animals or work with them. You want to be an engineer, a computer buff, a doctor, a nurse, or whatever. But still you *like* animals. You would like to know more about them or to help them. Or you love wild places and would like to make sure they stay wild and do not become polluted or get dug up for roads, houses, or shops.

It is very important to try to save wild places where wild, free animals live. Animals have just as much right to go on living their lives as we do. Also, if we destroy too much of the natural world, we shall be depriving those who live after us of much beauty.

It may be really disastrous for us to destroy some kinds of living things. We know that many important drugs used to cure human diseases come from plants or even from insects. When we destroy a wild area we may be destroying a whole species of plant or animal that is not found anywhere else. Without knowing it, we may be destroying the cure for cancer, or AIDS, or some other terrible disease.

In a forest, a desert, or any country area, all the different kinds of plants and animals make up a whole, wonderful, complex pattern. If we mess about with that pattern, all kinds of things can go wrong. For example, when the rabbits all over England died of the introduced rabbit disease, myxamotosis, the foxes didn't have much left to eat. So they began killing the farmers' chickens. The farmers then waged war against the foxes. And they found that the rats and mice multiplied, because there were no longer any foxes left to hunt them. The rats and mice destroyed the farmers' grain in the fields and in their stores. The farmers ended up losing as much, or more, of their crop to rodents as they had lost to the rabbits.

Consider the farmer who sprays his fields with insecticide to kill the bugs that are damaging his crops. He kills thousands of harmless insects as well, including some that actually do good—such as bees that pollinate the flowers and give us honey. Creatures that feed on insects, especially birds, also get sick and die. In the end, because the poisonous chemicals get widely distributed, humans may become sick, too.

There are so many ways in which animals are mistreated, many that people don't even know about. Or, if they do, they just think of it as something they can't do anything about. That's almost never true.

Think, for example, of the way most farm

117

animals are treated today. We call it "factory farming." Hens, in most parts of the western world, must live their lives squashed three (or more) together in very tiny cages. Pigs, who are as intelligent as most dogs, are crowded together in the same way, with no opportunity for rooting about in the mud or basking in the spring sunshine. There are still many farmers who treat their animals in the "old-fashioned" way, and you can still buy products from these farmers.

Thousands of animals are used every year for testing things such as detergent, cosmetics, and, in fact, almost every new product that comes on the market. Rabbits and guinea pigs, even dogs and cats, are used for this testing, as well as rats and mice. Sometimes the testing can cause the animal a lot of pain. Well, lots of people are fighting to change all this. Scientists, in particular, are working harder and harder to find out ways of testing substances without using animals.

Of course, many animals are used in medical research as well. This would not be quite so bad if all the research was useful and if the animals were treated really well. Unfortunately, a great amount of the research is of little or no use to humans, and in many cases the animals are treated very badly indeed. I shall talk more about this presently.

Why should we bother about the way animals

are treated? Does it matter? After all, there are a lot of humans who are very badly treated. Shouldn't we try to help them first? When people say this to me I find it quite easy to answer. Of course we must be concerned about badly treated people if we know about them. But so must we be concerned about badly treated animals, if we know about that. Cruelty is a terrible thing. I believe it is the worst human sin.

We are probably a long, long way from a world without cruelty. But I think we can all help, at least a little bit, to make it *less* cruel. We can all try to put right the things closest to home. If your neighbors are going out every evening and leaving their small son on his own, is that something to be worried about? Yes, of course it is. And what if your neighbors are mistreating their dog? Should you bother about that? I believe that you should. If the dog is being beaten, you can tell the local ASPCA. If the dog is left shut up for hours, you could offer, with your parents' permission, to take it for walks.

It is really important for animals that we speak our minds when we see something wrong. And that is not always easy. When I was about your age I once saw four boys, much bigger than I was, pulling the legs off crabs. I was very upset. I asked them why they did it, and they said, "None of your business." I told them it was cruel. They laughed.

And I went away. Now, forty years later, I am still ashamed of myself. Why didn't I try harder to stop them from tormenting those crabs?

I was not like my son. Once, when he was five years old, he was at a nursery school in California (at a time when I used to teach, one quarter a year, at Stanford University). One day he saw a seven-year-old boy hosing a terrified rabbit in its cage and laughing. Grub went up and tried to pull the hose away. The boy wouldn't let go, so Grub started a fight. And though he was much smaller, he managed to win.

The teacher was very angry with Grub and punished him. She didn't even punish the other boy for being cruel. But Grub, even though he was punished, knew he had done the right thing. He had stopped the tormenting of the rabbit.

Because I have spent so many years working with chimps, and because they are so like human beings, I am especially concerned by the terrible things that are happening to them. In all the places where they live in Africa, the forests are being cut down, partly so rich men can get richer by selling the timber, and partly because the Africans need more space. And the chimpanzees are being shot. They are shot for food. Mothers are shot so that hunters can steal their babies and sell them for medical research.

I want to help people raise money to save some

of the forests for the chimps and all the other animals that live there.

Because chimp bodies are so like human bodies, and because chimps can get all our diseases, hundreds are being used in our research labs to help scientists find cures or vaccines for human illnesses. And what is so awful is that these chimps are usually treated very badly (as badly as many other lab animals are) by people who don't care. The chimps are put into tiny cages, often by themselves, with nothing comfortable to sit on, nothing to play with, and no one to comfort and love them when they are hurt. If you do things like this to a human being, he or she goes mad. So do the chimps. I want to try to help them.

One day, perhaps quite soon, scientists may not need to use animals for testing drugs and for learning about human diseases. They are so clever at finding other ways of doing this.

But until that happens it is desperately urgent that we try to give those animals being used today much better places to live, much better care, much more respect, and much more love.

I'm going to end with a story. It's a story about a chimpanzee called Old Man. He was bought by a zoo in North America when he was an adolescent. We don't know his history. Perhaps he was once in a lab or a circus. But he hated people. He was put to live on an island with three grown-up females. He got on fine with them. And one of the females had a baby. Old Man was the father.

Just about that time, a young man called Marc got a job looking after the chimps. Marc's job was to paddle a boat out toward the island and throw food to the chimpanzees. Everyone told him how dangerous they were. And, truly, adult chimps in captivity usually are dangerous. Most of them have not been well treated.

For a while Marc fed the chimps the way he had been told to. Then he decided that he couldn't properly look after animals without some trust. So he began to make friends. He went closer and closer. He handed them their food. He said nice things to them. And at last he could get onto the island. At first the adults still attacked him sometimes, but even though he got bitten, Marc didn't give up.

He became friendly with Old Man, and he could play with him and groom him. But the three females were more standoffish.

One day Marc slipped and fell close to the infant. The infant screamed in fright, and at once the mother leapt onto Marc and began to bite his neck. He felt the blood run down. Before he could get up, the other two females also joined the attack. One bit his arm, one his leg. He felt his hand go numb. He thought that he had had it. He could never escape now.

Suddenly Old Man rushed up. He seized hold of the females, one after the other, and pulled them off Marc. He hurled them away. Marc began to drag himself toward the boat. Old Man stayed close beside him, threatening the females every time they tried to attack again. At last, Marc got off the island. Old Man had saved his life.

That story has taught me a lot. If a chimpanzee can reach out to help a human, then we humans can reach out and try to help the chimpanzees and all the other creatures we live with in the world today.

This is what I am trying to do. I hope you will help me.

The infant Flint reaching out to his human companion. Photograph by Hugo van Lawick, © National Geographic Society.

About the Author

Jane Goodall was born in London on April 3, 1934, and grew up in Bournemouth, on the southern coast of England. In 1960, she began studying chimpanzees in the wild in Gombe, Tanzania. After receiving her doctorate in Ethology at Cambridge University, Dr. Goodall founded the Gombe Stream Research Center for the study of chimpanzees and baboons. In 1975, she established the Jane Goodall Institute for Wildlife Research, Education and Conservation to promote animal research throughout the world. Dr. Goodall is well known for her contributions to several stunning *National Geographic* films and has written three books for adults, including the best-seller *In the Shadow of Man*. She has won many awards for her work, such as the Golden Medal of Conservation from the San Diego Zoological Society and the J. Paul Getty Wildlife Conservation Prize.

If you want to know more about Jane Goodall and her work with the chimpanzees, please write to: Jane Goodall Institute for Wildlife Research, Education and Conservation, P.O. Box 599, Ridgefield, CT 06877.